A Medium's Cookbook:
recipes for the soul

Suzane Northrop

NorthStar 2 LLC

A Medium's Cookbook:
recipes for the soul

**A Step-by-step guide toward creating
a Banquet of Connections
to those who have "passed over"**

Northstar 2 LLC
P.O. Box 870
New York, NY 10024
www.suzanenorthrop.com
Tel. 516-676-7036

Cover Design by Jennifer Ramsey
Interior Design by Eas Gooch
Photography of Suzane Northrop by Joe Henson

Editorial Supervision by Chad Edwards and Eleanor Honig-Skoller

CIP data available from the Library of Congress

ISBN 09762608-3-2

08 07 06 05   4 3 2 1
First printing, October 2005

Printed in the United States of America

Aaron

You are forever in my heart

Contents

Preface

In a day and age when we are seemingly besieged by the media's interpretations in some form or other about messages from beyond, it is necessary that we come to understand what is real, what is fiction, what is possible, and what we can do about creating our own connections with those who have passed over, doing our own healing, and finding our truths. I have often become disturbed by the portrayals of mediums on such TV programs and series as *The Medium, The Ghost Whisperer*, TV news specials, and magazine and newspaper articles. But, when I take a moment to breathe and release, I realize that at least these media products are causing exposure to making contact and conversations about it, as well as promoting questions about what is really true and possible. And, that's a good thing. TV and other media start us wondering. These presentations sometimes give us a degree of insight into how it is to live with such a "gift" on a daily basis as we interact with family, friends, and co-workers. We get a chance to observe how one who has such a *calling* is affected, and how it alters the lives of those around them. Having had this calling from an early age, I find that it is not necessarily something I would have chosen. Yet, as the years have progressed, it has become a part of me for which I am truly grateful. It is a good thing to help people heal. What we need now, however, is guidance toward what is real about what we are being exposed to in the world concerning *connecting* to the "other side." Whether you have a sense that you have been connecting, and/or you have the desire to learn ways to enhance your connections, this book will help give you a better understanding of what is possible to do and how to go about doing it.

It is likely that part of the reason you are drawn to this book is that you have some unresolved issue with a loved one who has passed, one that remains unsettling for *YOU.* Maybe you have come here because you have heard of my work, and that has sharpened your interest. If you are drawn here, most likely it is because something in your soul, and quite possibly something connected with a loved one who has *passed over,* is probably nagging at you. There may have been some "happenings" which have given you an indication that your loved one is here, around you, and wants you to know something. If so, more than anything, it is about *their* love for you, and their desire to help with *your* healing. Those on the other side are healed already.

I have said this a zillion times, but to reiterate it just once more, my work is about the *living* not the dead—and so is *your* work. Our DPs—my identification for dead people—are just fine and they want nothing more than to let you know just that. But with us, the living, all underlying unresolved issues become heightened when a loved one dies. The more complicated the death, the more unsettled we remain. It all comes to the surface, and it is we who have to do the healing—not them. They are "connecting" in order to assist you. In my years of experience doing this work, most people want me to do it for them—to make that connection for them. I am honored to do that, however, the truth of the matter is that the healing process will affect you emotionally and physically, and dealing with grief or an unresolved issue is a journey, one of healing the wounds and losses of separation which can be done *only* by you! Only you can walk your path, only you can feel the particular pain you feel, and, by the same token, only you can block the very healing that you desire. This is *your* soul's journey, and no one else's. Be courageous, and you'll be amazed at the "life shifts" that are possible. Since this is an on-going process—in all honesty, there are deaths we will never completely get over—and by courageously walking this path, you might just face some of your deepest fears and learn more keenly the importance of your *own* life. Keep in mind, the word "courage" lies in the base of the heart.

In preparing the approach to this book, I came upon the idea of a cookbook and the recipes we follow to create magnificent meals that are nourishing and nurturing. I recalled the atmospheres that were created—sometimes good, sometimes not—when seated around the table. I had memories of how I was told about preparing and creating the dishes. I thought about the ingredients we must have for the recipes to work. Those thoughts gave way to old familiar family "recipes" that I have carried with me for years—one was, "don't mess with a 'sure' thing, whether you like it or not." I asked, "Why not?" *Is there an explorer in you?*

All of the questions and pictures that came to me around cookbooks, ingredients, recipes, and the effects a sumptuous meal can have, gave rise to my excitement when I saw the connection with how we could go about preparing ourselves to connect and heal. It's like selecting the best that we have access to in order to achieve the best outcome. It is our choice to make—or we can do it with a bit of support. So, I am about to offer you some of the best recipes that have gone into my own personal banquets over the years. I am excited to pull from my own "pantry" many ingredients that have proven themselves to support my path, my soul's journey. I also want to call attention to the things that have gotten in the way —the blocks that may still be sitting on the back shelf with a "use by" date that is long past and that still remains in the way of *your* soul's healing.

Therefore, as we proceed, I will use the analogy of cookbooks, recipes, ingredients and tools to make our process appear to be as much as a part of life as possible. I think you will fall in step with my approach as we go along. It also gives a lighter edge to the learning and understanding of how we can enhance our own connections and healings, and what we do to hinder or stop them. By no means, is it my intention to be frivolous about something so important to our lives. But most, I find, get way too serious about something that is truly *wonderful*. It is my desire that you "put on your apron, get the appropriate ingredients, and tools and cook your own recipes" for your journey's success. This is about waking up the "inner-cook" in you.

It seems to be the season to plant those seeds for your garden that begin to create your own recipes. Isn't that why you are here? You just may find out that what your soul is about to learn may bring an extra bushel of sweet fruits to your life. These *recipes* are offered to help you learn that the quality of life—your personal banquet—does not evolve by accumulating things, but in peeling away the layers to reveal the essentials that bring value to your soul. I've condensed a lifetime of connecting trial and error experiences to assist you in finding your own inner peace.

Come, and step into *my* kitchen. The banquet awaits you.

Blessings,
Suzane

Acknowledgments

I have had the honor and privilege for over thirty years to work in a profession in which daily I feel blessed. Yes, there have been those moments of frustration and hurt, yet after all these years, I still feel it all has given me a very special life. It has been a privilege to connect in a way to that very personal and private part of someone that not many get to share. For that, I'm truly grateful. Even in a crowded room, those precious moments that are shared by those who really care to understand and witness the connection to a loved one or DP that has gone before us are extraordinary.

Throughout the years, and over many miles of travel, I have joyously had the opportunity to connect with many new associates that have not only been peers professionally, but have become treasured friends as well. Just to name a few—Gary Craig of WTIC in Hartford, CT, a better friend, I could never ask for; Bob Wolf, WPYX, New York, an incredible risk-taker; Ellen Z, who constantly shares her skills and friendship; WXLO in MA, Jen, Chris, and Steve, thanks for your on-going support; Ross Britain, The Breakfast Club, WOGL Philadelphia, PA, who believes deeply in helping along the way, always giving back; Art Sears, a constant from the beginning; Gary Bernstein, who remains committed to going all the way; Rick Martini, for taking a chance; Blaine Ensley and Michelle Vargas of WNEW in NY, for New York, New York, you're spreading the news!

Chad Edwards, "my voice," who reaches beyond my expectations—you made this book happen. I'll be forever thankful. You are truly the "book doctor."

Eleanor Honig-Skoller—your brilliance as an editor shines to reflect how very special your talents are—never let them go unnoticed. You are my family.

And, of course, kudos to "The Dream Team." To name a few—Dennis McMahon, a steady force filled with caring, and the board you've protected like your baby; Molly Wentworth, you brought the newsletter to light; Gretchen Harb, you hold the mike like no one can. And, for the numerous special people who are always there to help, you add so much that many may not notice, but I do. You know what giving without expecting is all about. After all, it is the special ones in the background who end up on the front lines when help is truly needed! Last, but not least, a big thanks to Jess Steinman for all you do and care for as part of the "team".

To my sister Cindy, who together we weathered that awful storm. I love you.

To my mother for having the strength to go on through all the difficulties life has presented. I love you.

Through the years, I have continued to be supported by so many I call friends—time is always the greatest testament to friends. Some of you are Deborah, Pat, and Jodelle Dearmin, The Hetricks, my second family, Billy Degan, Dr. Bridget Duffy, Terry Platz, Jim Platz, Susan Gross, Libby Jordan, Nick Newmont, John Holland, Rauni King, Bobby Manning, James Manning, Dr Mimi Guarneri, Meg Zinc, and Faith Busby. If I have not mentioned you, know you are there in my thoughts.

Linda Manning, who is not only an amazement to me, but to everyone who comes in contact with her. She truly touches souls she doesn't even know. I am honored to have her along with me. No one cares more. Thank you for all you do.

I would like to acknowledge and thank every guest on my radio show who gave so much, and for graciously sharing your time and expertise around your work to my listeners—there are far too many to mention, but you know who you are.

Aileen, you're my rock, confidant, friend, and partner. You've taken *Northstar 2,* cradled it like a baby, and given it your all. I am touched by your strength to see things through. Thank you, you have always made the world a better place. You have shown me what commitment and integrity should be in friendships and partnerships.

As always, I am touched by those loving DPs that embrace my life. You have shown me what love truly is as you work so hard to let us know in the physical world. You have taught me that it really is about love, and yes, that love is immortal.

Section One

Preparation
— First Things First

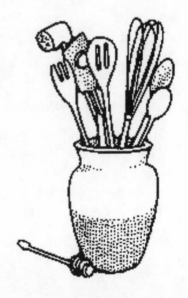

CHAPTER ONE:
What to Understand Before You Enter the "Kitchen"

So, you are interested in learning how to make a connection with a loved one who has *passed over.* That's great! Are you also ready to do some personal "soul healing?" For that is really why you are here—to make your Soul Program. For many of us, the loss of a loved one brings up our innermost beliefs and attitudes about death. The way we feel about death is often a reflection of how we view life itself. Many of us have been strongly influenced in the way we think about the idea of an existence after death by our upbringing. We may find ourselves asking, "Is there life-after-death, or is this life a one-time shot? Could this be just one part of a much larger and on-going journey? Am I actually making contact or am I just making it up out of wishful thinking?"

Just as I had in the beginning, some of you may have a great many questions about the afterlife. While I appreciate the fact that I've been given the special gift of having a heightened ability to tune into the vibrations of those in the world of spirit, I also have come to understand that each of you also has the capacity to enhance your own abilities to connect with that world. The one thing you must always remember is that the DPs *want* to make the connection. In fact, it's a major part of their *job* to connect with you. Your job is to open your heart and mind as you learn to listen in this broader sense. If you don't do that, the messages may go unnoticed, and you'll be depriving yourself of the peace and comfort that comes from knowing your departed loved ones are not only alright, but are also still very much connected to you. Because you must want to do it very deeply, making a connection isn't always easy. There may be obstacles in the belief system with which you were raised that may make you skeptical or fearful of this kind of contact. You cannot allow any negative energy to enter your realm of being unless you *choose* to allow it in. I don't believe that any loved one who has passed over ever returns with anger or the desire to harm us. They are only about love. If you can resolve those doubts and fears that you have been taught to have, and come to believe that you *can* do this, you'll be preparing yourself to hear whatever messages the DPs need to send—even if they bring up issues or thoughts that might be disturbing to you. Such disturbances occur only because you carry or cling to some energy concerning the issues that haven't been understood or resolved yet. Sometimes these revolve around not forgiving yourself or others in your life, or those who have passed on. Remember, DPs don't carry resentment, fear, or anger. *They* have moved on. Most are in a state of joy, happiness, and compassion.

Your job is to open your heart and mind as you learn to listen in this broader sense.

As you consider making your own connections, there is something as a professional I need to explain. If you have attended a workshop, session, or speaking engagement guided by a medium, your contact in these cases most likely will be quite different from when you are making the attempt on your own. Why? Because the loved one has to use a more "in your face" and recognizable action with the medium to get your attention. The DP would continue to have a specific personality trait, especially when they are coming through to someone like me in my setting, so they can exhibit a specific identification for someone in the room.

Although they are brought over from a place of love, their

personalities often remain the same until their consciousness becomes balanced. Our consciousness is very different *with* the body than without it. So, please be aware that if someone had an unsettling or nasty personality trait here on earth, or caused harm to someone or suffered a less-than-pleasant death, it doesn't mean that he or she will become immediately changed when they pass over. If a loved one was a bit stubborn or controlling on this side, he or she most likely will come through to me with that same personality trait. They may stay within that mindset until they become aware they are not in the physical body, and their actions come into balance with their karma—a basic law of the Universe. When you begin working to make contact on your own, your "hints" of validation of a DP's presence can be amazingly different. You can experience a much "softer" means of identification.

However many souls are trying to get a word in, it's usually the ones with the strongest, most determined personalities (and they are usually the ones who were that way in life) whose messages come through first. The quiet, shrinking violets just have to wait their turn—but will get it. Again, this is more prevalent with my work. It is not under our control, but the DPs seem to have arranged it so that no one gets shut out.

Communicating with the DPs is not like holding a normal conversation. You can't just ask them questions and get back answers in complete, cohesive sentences. Sometimes you will just receive a word or even a strong physical sensation. I must also caution you that we never see DPs directly—*always peripherally*. That is not to say that people do not see DPs, it is just that *appearing* is their least desired form of connection. The

DPs communicate chiefly through dreams because the right brain is more in the foreground when you are relaxed and there is no interference. Another reason is that in the dream state, you are not startled by their appearance as you would be if they just showed up when you were awake. Other favorite ways the DPs communicate are via music, children, animals, and smells. Most often they will make contact with you when you are engaged in nonlinear activities—when the left brain is in the background. They come through often when one is in the car listening to the radio—and through computers as well. For most of us though, our main desire for connection with the ones who have passed is due to what we want or need to say, do, or resolve.

There is a book that I am reminded of called, "The Lovely Bones" by Alice Sebold. In it, a young girl is brutally raped and murdered. After passing over, the young girl, Susie, begins to *speak* to the readers from heaven, where she says "life is a perpetual yesterday." From this vantage point, she narrates and keeps watch over her grieving family and friends, as well as her brazen killer and the sad detective working on her case. It is a moving exploration of loss and mourning that ultimately puts its faith in the living. She's growing up on the other side, and watching her family and the "guy" go through their processes. She is not involved directly, but is present in love.

There was a recent incident here in the U.S. where a family was brutally murdered and two of the children, a brother and sister, abducted. The murderer, a registered sex-offender, ultimately killed the boy. I believe that for some reason the boy sacrificed his life, passing over, in order to save the sister. Fortunately, she was recognized in a restaurant by a waitress, and rescued, the murderer taken into custody. I feel that the brother had a hand in the rescue from the spirit world.

If you are willing to get ready, if you are resolved, free of fear, and steady in your own belief system, then I would like to help you by sharing some of the methods I teach people who come to my workshops. I will show you how you can begin a practice that just might lead you to a connection with one who has passed over. Many of you may be getting some signals or messages already, and you are wondering if what you are experiencing has happened to anyone else. You may start questioning the reality of what is going on, you may begin to wonder if your imagination has gone a bit wild. This is enough to keep you silent about what you are experiencing for fear of being ridiculed. One of the strongest hindrances to

> ### *You no longer need to feel helpless when someone you love dies.*

the spiritual evolution of human beings is that so many have been taught to believe that this one lifetime is the sum of our complete existence. We think that when we are dead we cease to exist, thus, we are never drawn to imagine there could be a greater purpose to our lives. Perhaps you have been asking some of the tougher questions of yourself and challenging your beliefs because you are grieving over the death of someone very close to you. Perhaps you would like to resolve issues around his or her departure and accept the gift of knowledge that the DP in your life may bring you in your effort to answer your soul's true questions. This practice you are about to embark on is for those who wish to explore contact with any loved one in the afterlife, no matter how or when they departed this plane.

What you will find here is—a committed practice—that will become a place in which you can explore the greater purpose of your soul, and learn ways to increase your sensitivity to the unseen parts of your world, the Universe, and your existence. If you have made the decision, or are in the process of making the decision, something in you has drawn you to joining those of us who wish to expand our life's recipes and start "cooking on all burners." You no longer need to feel helpless when someone you love dies.

What this "cookbook" is really about is *LOVE*. The DPs can't walk your path but they can help you walk it. The folks that have passed over are not focused the way we are about their death. They love you and want you to know that, and they want you to heal yourself. They are supposed to let you know about this "connection" anyway they can in order to help you through your healing process. Once again let me say, they can't walk our path, but they are there to help us walk it.

The purpose of this book and my life's work as a teacher and trance medium, is to help you make the connections that are necessary for you to help you do your own work. My work, then, is different from those psychics who work on crimes because I may not obtain specific information about a situation. But because we each work differently, there are exceptions to this. As a rule, however, it is the psychic who works with police and who will "pick up" information or clues about the crime to support the investigation and its resolution.

I have had the privilege of studying and working with one of the first psychics to have gotten a badge with the Orange County California Police Department. Betty Sittauer was highly respected

and worked on the "Hillside Strangler" case in Los Angeles, one of the biggest in history. It was the early 70s, and psychics were not getting credit in those days for their work, and few police investigators would admit to working with them. She was not a medium, but a superb psychic. When working on a case, Betty would receive what she called a "print out." The only information the police would give her would be a name. She would follow her "print out,"

There are many ways to explore the making of connections.

and then the police would follow the leads she got. Never once, did I hear Betty say she was getting this information from the DPs. Combining psychics and mediums as if there were no differences between them is confusing those who watch Hollywood generated productions around psychic detective work. Hollywood embellishes their products to make things entertaining and to draw the viewer in. That's their business. Mediums are about connecting to loved ones, not finding perpetrators of crimes.

Having said all this, of course there are exceptions. Generally, a medium does not work like a psychic. The connections we make are with those who are not concerned with the how or the why of their passing. We know the DPs are where they are supposed to be, and that they want only to let those they left behind to know that they are okay and that they are loved. The work I do is about helping you make the connections to those loved ones—and I cannot think of a better way than to teach you how to begin to do that yourselves. This work is about tuning up your antennae in order to be able *to listen and to hear* those messages that can be helpful, in so many different ways, to your healing.

Creating certain bonds in our lives have no doubt been behind the countless organizations that have been born of tragic deaths or human suffering. Take note of just a few: UNICEF, the American Red Cross, MADD, Nicole Brown [Simpson] Charitable Foundation, and Compassionate Friends. Where there is death, a cause often arises. These are mass events that in the end affect our individual soul's journey, making the connection among us strong, indeed. By picking up this book and contemplating the task of enhancing your ability to "connect," you have already started on a path of expanded consciousness. It will be a personal journey. Above all, as we proceed, it is important to avoid the urge to compare yourself to anyone else or to wonder why another may seem to progress faster than you. Each of us is unique, and so is our path toward enlightenment. Remember, just as there are differences between the TV chefs on the Food Network, *Emeril* and *Paula's Home Cooking,* each in their own way is successful because they stay with what they know well—their own way of cooking.

There are many ways to explore the making of connections. So, I ask you to leave your expectations in the refrigerator. Allow them to chill for a while. If you get rooted in expectation, you may unconsciously begin to set up blocks to your progression. For our purposes in learning to connect, find that place in you that gives permission to the soul to open up to the countless levels of possibilities. Coming from that place, you may be surprised at what you are able to accomplish. Some days you may have great results, and some days not, but remember it is usually the little things that unveil the epiphanies. Without realizing it, you will be led down a path of examining the input you have received from your parents, grandparents, life relationships, as well as the choices you have made that have created your beliefs. You will eventually come to decide whether those belief systems are working for you now—and if not, how you might change them. You will be probing the overt and covert messages you received while growing up that are directing your life. As you probably realize, the messages we received about not speaking were quite often the most powerful: *don't* talk about feelings, *don't* question, *don't* argue, *don't* show emotions, and so on. During this process it's not what we have to learn as much as it's what we have to *unlearn:* indiscriminate dependence on critical thinking, too much stress placed on analysis, and the use of the fallacy of objectivity, among others. It is time to soften the hard edges of "this-is-so," and "that-is-not-so."

We are also going to be working on balancing the right and left parts of the brain—the intuitional and rational balance of ourselves. For most of us, this involves *both* turning up the volume on the intuitive, and turning it down on the rational. And in saying this, I don't mean to imply that rational thought has no place in the world—of course it does. It should not, however, take up *all* the places in the world. Rationality becomes a prison when it becomes the only way to understand how things are. There is no more desolate picture than one of a lonely person who is convinced that this life is all there is, and that death is annihilation. But there is another picture. You can learn to meet your loved ones at the banquet table, raise your glass overflowing with the "wine of life," and toast your good fortune in not choosing on-going "heartburn," but, the soothing delight of continuing your adventure.

In short, we have to do some work to begin to make the connections we desire. DPs don't have the physical difficulties that they had prior to their passing, and they don't have the same kind of emotions that they had in the physical form. They come to bring messages of reassurance that they are doing well, and often, bring suggestions and information for those of us on *this side* that help to heal unresolved relationship issues. They come to offer you assistance, but definitely not to make decisions for you. They won't interfere with your path, they may, however, send you a "signal" to take notice of something that is about to happen that may not be in your best interest. They realize that ultimately it is still *your* life—and that the choices are yours. Those in the next life look at how busy we are, refusing commitment, denying responsibility, throwing off blame, all because the truth often pinches. So much goes unhealed. The DPs come to know all of this instantly when they cross over.

Keep in mind that children and animals are the greatest "connectors"

The voices I hear come from loved ones who have passed over. They have finished this lifetime's roles, work, issues, and have the rest of their journey to get on with. They are taking time out from their own paths to reach back spiritually and touch us. They are making the time, borrowing a moment from infinity to ask us to listen and to let them help. That is why it is so important that we do our work on this side.

DPs help us find truths we never knew. It is their responsibility to get us the necessary message, through whatever means possible—and the message can come in a myriad of ways. Once you get a "message," it is imperative that you listen. That is your responsibility: to listen, be open, to trust, and to know you have been in communication with your loved ones. The DPs, who have had time to think about things, believe the living need to hear some hard truths. Their messages are not about themselves, but about us—and they bring them with some urgency. They want to show us how to be happy in *this* life.

DPs are relentless about getting through, and will stay with something until we get it. Communicating with DPs is not like holding a normal conversation in which a question is asked and an answer is given. Sometimes it is only a word or even a strong physical sensation that is sent. You may catch a whiff of a favorite perfume, a prized cigar, the acrid aroma of the two-pack-a-day smoker. Anywhere and everywhere we must learn to be open to the communications. Keep in mind that children and animals are the greatest "connectors" mostly because they are not imprinted with the judgments and biases with which we have been conditioned.

There are many rewards that may be attained when given a second chance with someone you know that has passed over and is now living in the spirit world. Quite often, after someone we know dies, we are left with unfinished business involving that person, making our lives seem incomplete and unsettled. Isn't that why you are here, reading? If it's because you want to become a professional medium, you are "cooking" in the wrong kitchen. The practice laid out here is about taking you through the process necessary to make contact with those you know in the spirit world, allowing you a second chance to do your healing and find resolution. This is about continuing your Soul Program, not about becoming a medium.

I have created this course of practice and discovery for anyone who desires to get in touch with a higher truth of connection, and to better understand the "oneness" of all things in the Universe. If you can come to believe that death is not the end, you will release potential within yourself. Because you have made the decision to be here, reading this book, I know you have the desire to discover that potential. What I offer here is a collection of powerful concepts to contemplate, a call to examine your beliefs, to engage with lessons and exercises to find the ingredients that will help you develop your ability to connect on a deeper level with those who reside on the other side—*and with yourself.*

Now is the time for you to lay claim to the "Master Chef" in you. The one who decides upon, and orchestrates the most magnificent banquet the soul has to offer. I also encourage you to let go of any preconceived notions about making contact with your loved ones as you begin to explore the processes offered in this book.

Here are some points to remember as we start this journey toward connecting: you must always keep your link to the "who" of who you are—your essence. Be honest.

Practice patience. In most cases, keep the process simple and try not to be too hard on yourself.

No matter where you come from, or where you are going at any given moment, you will still be under some degree of influence from your "roots"—life's input into your belief systems. These roots will have an impact on the "recipes" you choose from the cookbooks and the menus you are getting ready to create—especially, in the beginning.

Risks are part of the exploration process, and from whatever level of risk-taking that you are comfortable with, most assuredly, you will be asked to stretch yourself to become an explorer.

When faced with the need for an instantaneous response, remember your basic essence will emerge.

Be selective about with whom you share your innermost thoughts and your progress in the program. Remember in sharing these thoughts, there are those whose fears can get in the way.

Do what works for you.

To keep your progress on track, it is always prudent to maintain a degree of privacy.

No matter how quickly you may feel you are progressing with this work, remember *sous chefs* work their way up. One does not become a top chef immediately.

Don't get bogged down trying to create the "perfect awesome meal." Give yourself a break and create your menu on the lighter side. Eating in diners instead of starred restaurants is fine for many people.

Above all, allow this to be a journey of pleasure, joy, and adventure for you. If it doesn't become one, then also give yourself permission to put it aside for the time being, or to reach out to a professional for support.

As you go through the book, you will find exercises to try: some for journaling, some for reflection, and some that will call for action. Also, at the end of each chapter, you will find "Recipe Cards" that are provided to help you anchor the information I have presented in the chapter before you move on. You will want to keep a few different journals throughout, (more explanation on journals is found in Chapter Six), and you will want to keep them in a safe place. These journals will become your "friends and confidants," and you will want to be as honest as possible in them about what you are feeling and experiencing. What you write is for your growth and for your eyes only. Journaling is a most personal activity. Later on, if you wish, you can share what you have written. Obviously, there will be times when you feel you don't have the time or desire to do every exercise. Do what works for you. You can do as little or as much depending on what resonates with your *own* soul's journey.

Happy Connecting—with yourself, and your loved ones!

RECIPE CARD:

 Write a page about why you desire to connect with the DPs in your life, about what brought you to this effort.

 Have you ever had the opportunity to contact a DP? Write about who it was and what you experienced. Always be sure to state your feelings regarding your contact and what messages you believe you have received.

CHAPTER TWO:
What's in Your Pantry?
What are You Bringing to the Table?

I mpressions from the table

As we begin to explore the "family recipes," that is, what we are bringing to the "table of our existence," we must widen our search for clarity regarding *why you are here*. The questions that might have brought you to this moment might be "Why am I here on earth?" or "Why am I here reading this book?" or even "Why do I want to make contact with the DPs?" If you are here to answer any of these, you are also here to expand your soul's journey. These questions and impressions will be a strong influence on how you proceed with your learning and practice. They will give you some indication about how open *or* closed you are to the new ideas and concepts. For instance, were "family recipes"—your beliefs—sacred and untouchable, or could you change them to suit your taste? What significance do your traditional recipes hold for you? A key question to ask is, "Are you afraid to change a "recipe"—a belief that has been passed down through the generations?" What emotions arise when you think about "tinkering" with the tried and true ingredients of such a recipe? These kinds of questions help to create a beneficial investigation into just how comfortable we are with taking risks, and with the feelings that emerge when we begin to embrace the adventurer, the explorer in ourselves.

Many of us have vivid memories of coming to the family table for a meal. Some of us conjure up memories of pleasant, even joyful times, while others of us do not. There may have been a lot of turmoil in your family, and coming to the table to share a meal was an event you dreaded. Maybe you were expected to attend the meal in silence. Eventually, you may have found any excuse to avoid being there. I am sure that if you work on recalling those times, tangible emotions will arise. There are questions you can

19

ask yourselves to prompt the recollections: were tables set with great thought and flair, or were they sparse and unappealing? Were there cloth napkins and tablecloths? Was the table set neatly or without much care? Was the meal a time for the family to come together and share thoughts and experiences, or was it hurried without any sense of connection among you—get in, eat, and get out?

In today's world, some of our moments might be shared over a meal at some "Fast Food" place out of necessity, especially among single mothers or families on the run. Here, too, we find the same dynamics appearing as they do at the table at home. I'm sure that the kind of energy circulating in the family unit will be expressed at any of these tables.

Emotional anchors are created around the atmosphere that permeates the coming together for a meal. Remembering these settings will bring you some insight into your beliefs about being nourished. Were you asked to participate in creating the meal, setting the table, and did everyone take part in cleaning up? For instance, my mother did not allow us to help with cooking the meal, but expected us to do the cleaning afterwards. In my family, the siblings were all girls, and you might think that we would have been taught the artistry of preparing a meal in order to help us to become good spouses and mothers. No, not at all! Now, to no one's surprise, I don't cook.

Another important question to ask ourselves is how we feel about breaking with tradition. Many of us have certain rituals around eating that come from our various cultures, and there are, as well, the different foods that are indicative of our heritages. What were (and what are) your thoughts about this?

Did you enjoy it, or were there foods you didn't care for, and *had* to eat time after time? It is important to examine this because it can give you some indication of your willingness to step out and try something new. Different kinds of foods can bring different experiences. It is also interesting, I think, to look at how often your food changed—if it ever did. If you happen to be in a family that regularly ate the same things over and over, it might signal that your parents had a degree of rigidity around change. Were you that way, too? On the other hand, you may have been in a family that loved to explore new tastes and recipes. How do you think that would affect your ability to explore?

A variety of attitudes and behaviors exist around the table in all cultures, but in those that are different from ours, the way a meal is experienced, may be unfamiliar to us and have different resonances. Some who have married outside their cultures go through many changes— some emotional—when faced with the introduction of foods

> **There was no message ever given that it was important to be together to nourish either their bodies or their souls.**

and food preparation they are not used to. Has that happened to you and how has it affected you? There are quite a number of "belief anchors" created around the way a family or culture approaches food and mealtimes. What are some in your family of origin?

I remember a friend of mine from South Dakota who married an Italian man from New York. His grandmother moved in with them to teach my friend, the "non-Italian," how to cook pasta. She remembers the battles they had, and throwing the pasta against the wall—clearly, not a good ethnic connection

for her! She still has nightmares about this and has spent a good deal of money on therapy because of it.

I knew a Greek fellow in my neighborhood who never spoke English. He would go out to his yard and garden, pick "things" from the ground, bring them in the house, throw them in a pot with some other ingredients, and cook it. I always thought that was interesting. God knows what it was or what was in it, but he kept that pot boiling all day. That was so different from what went on in my house. I think that I'm drawn to different cultures and foods to this day because of my curiosity about that pot.

A friend once shared with me that his family would only come to the table "on the run." There was never any thought of coming together at the same time, sharing a meal, or engaging in conversation about what was going on in their lives. His mother never sat at the table with them. She prepared the meal, eating as she went along, and then sat at the counter, watching them eat from afar. Also, this family had a running account at a local eatery where they could go and have a meal—breakfast, lunch, or dinner—whenever they were hungry. There was no message ever given that it was important to be together to nourish either their bodies or their souls. On the rare occasions when they did sit down to a meal together, all they did was to quickly ingest something and move on. To this day, my friend has a hard time sitting down at a table for a leisurely meal with family or friends—but he is working on it, he tells me.

Did your family ever go out to dine? If so, did you go to the same place each time, or did it vary, adding some sense of adventure to dining? Were you encouraged to order what you wanted or expected to choose the same thing every time? Are there certain foods or dishes that you label "comfort foods," those you turn toward when you are in need of some nurturing? What is it about them that gives you a feeling of comfort? And are they really nourishing, or are they merely numbing your emotions? Also, if you had some obsessive eating conditioning when you were young, you might be approaching the work we are doing here obsessively as well. That doesn't work. You will never get to where you want to go or to what you want to achieve if you are narrowly focused

Holidays bring up the deepest pain in relation to loss.

on the obsession. Obsessing is like being on a treadmill that you can't get off. People on diets are good examples of this. Many obsessively try one diet after another and then find they don't work. We now know they don't work because they have not allowed healthy eating to become *a way of life.* They are obsessive about a diet plan and on losing weight when they should be working on making changes in their lives for long-term overall benefits. Your process here is not only about "getting there," but mostly about paying attention to the journey as you move along.

Sometimes our religious backgrounds create beliefs that are anchored to sharing a meal together. There might have been certain foods that were not to be eaten at all or only at certain times. If that was the case for you, did you ever break with that tradition? Did you do it openly, or secretively? How did you feel about that? Were you ever sent away from the table—a place that is supposed to be about nurturing and nourishing? If so, did it give you a feeling of being abandoned? Did that leave you with

23

a resistance to joining in family meals, or an aversion toward participating in the preparation of them?

Holidays and celebrations such as birthdays are, for some, probably layered with the most intense reflections about "the table" and may have left deep imprints on emotions and beliefs. Thoughts around these gatherings can bring up all levels of connection *and* disconnection. Holidays bring up the deepest pain in relation to loss. Were there any holiday rituals celebrated in your family? Do you recall certain celebrations that had an impact on you and how you think about them today? Were they a joyous time, fun-filled, and something you anticipated or did you dread them? How have they affected the beliefs you have now?

Someone I know told me about a surprise birthday party that was given for her. There had been a huge fight—a frequent occurrence in that household—between the parents earlier that day which had traumatized her and she just wanted to be alone for her birthday. After a rousing argument with her mother in the car driving home from her Dad's office, she arrived to find a large group of friends waiting to surprise her with a party. Of course, she had been crying and was terribly embarrassed to have her friends see her unsettled and red-eyed. As a result, even today, she does not like birthday parties given for her or surprises. She cannot handle the attention given to her or the event. There are too many negative associations that come into recall. Oddly enough, she rarely misses celebrating other's.

> **If you think you were contacted, you probably were.**

I remember one family birthday party where I decided to make a cake as a surprise. Not having been encouraged to cook or explore, I ended up using baking soda instead of baking powder in the cake. No more baking for me! You can imagine the ridicule that set into motion! If you are afraid of "not doing it right" or you are not supposed to talk to the dead because of religious or other instilled suggestions, then you will have to work very hard to get started and even to make connections.

Examining our beliefs around connecting

Again we start with some questions: do you believe you *can* connect? What have you heard about people who claim to have made connections to those on the other side?

Most people have preconceived ideas about connecting with the dead: "this is bunk," "it's like Hollywood," "it's evil," or "you can only connect if you are *gifted*." Connections are not dramatic; don't look for

. . . the goal of communication is for your soul's growth, and not just for the sake of communicating.

the "Hollywood" approach. Most contacts are subtle, often quiet and to the point, and can be made through dreams, signs, and music, to mention only a few ways. They don't have to be made through something visible. If you think you were contacted, you probably were. If a loved one is still appearing to you as sick or angry, it's your own fears and unhealed issues—not theirs—that are cropping up showing you this image. Many of you experienced having "special gifts" as a child, only to have had them fade or discredited as you became adults. This book should help point you toward a path of reconnection to those parts of

you that have been abandoned. It will also help to change your beliefs about what you *can* do.

Expectations and beliefs lead to inventories

Developing the ability to have contact with those in the afterlife may not meet certain expectations you may have—remember in Chapter One we said that we are leaving those in the refrigerator. Sometimes we cannot help having expectations, but we can make an effort to recognize them ahead of time, enabling us to spot them when we find ourselves resorting to them instinctively.

In order to temper your expectations and put the possibilities on the "table," I would like you to complete the following inventory I have created for you. It will assist you to reach a deeper understanding of the reasons you want to do this work, and who you expect to contact. This inventory will help you identify every person you know who has passed, as well as any contacts you will *eventually* make. This process could very well reveal that you have already been contacted without being aware of it. It should also show you where your resistances dwell. Keep in the forefront of your consciousness that the goal of communication is for your soul's growth, and not just for the sake of communicating.

The Inventory

- Make a list of every person you know who has passed.
- Below each name, write down the date they passed and nature of your relationship with them.
- Also write a few sentences for each one that sums up your perception of his or her philosophy in life. If possible, distill

these into one or two phrases, for example, something he or she said repeatedly, something that might be positive or negative. These might be such phrases as "When life gives you lemons…" "If the shoe fits…" or "Everything happens for a reason."

What were each one's passions in life? Write at least two for each name.

Write down your most vivid memory of each person. Be as descriptive as you can.

Review this list, and ask yourself, "With whom do I want to have contact the *most*? Why?" "With whom do I want to have contact the *least*? Why?"

Keep this list handy so you can refer to it when you start having contacts. It can help jog your memory if a particular contact has you stumped. A good place to write all of this down is in a journal that you will use throughout this process. It doesn't have to be anything elaborate, but you can do what you want with to make it yours. We will talk about being artful with our journals later on. It might be helpful to use at *least* one page per name in case you want to add some thought or experience to a particular name as you go along. The whole purpose of the process is to encourage thoughts, memories and feelings to come up, and to recognize these more easily and more knowingly when they do.

I do not want to ignore the fact that there are many who have had wonderful experiences around the kitchen, cooking, the table, and meals. There are some recipes that bring us back to happy times. I still crave my grandmother's prune cookies every

Christmas. One of my holiday treats is dressing or stuffing, as it is sometimes called, and since I don't cook, I have made sure that my friends know just how to cook it like my mother does—and not stuffed inside the bird since I don't eat meat or fowl. It is still a "must have" delight from a great family recipe. I remember a set of sisters whose father made wine, and they had great memories of being around him, especially while he was making it. After he died they went down to the cellar and had a hell of a good time celebrating him.

I am sure that each of us can come up with a few great experiences. Some of us may have begun developing new atmospheres around the concept of "coming to the table" by creating new extended families, cooking up our own meals and setting our tables the way we want. The choice to celebrate our connections through the recipes we are about to create is ours. Our beliefs about what we can or cannot do are open to change if we allow it. It is time for us to examine the beliefs we have, and decide if they are still working for us. Maybe we won't throw them out completely like food that has gone bad, we can save what was good and mix it up with something new.

It is time for you, as your own "Chef of Connections," to come to the kitchen with the ingredients you choose, create the menu, cook, and set your table. You might very well be bringing to your table issues, beliefs, perceptions, judgments/biases, influences, resistances, and preconceived ideas about connecting that might be outdated. How willing are you to look at these things and make changes? Will we ultimately change all of our conceptions? Not necessarily. What we can do, however, is adjust our patterns and beliefs so that they work for us.

RECIPE CARD:

 List the beliefs you hold.

 Do any of your beliefs get in the way of making a connection? Which ones?

 In the form of a letter (be sure to date it), write two paragraphs to the person or persons about what has inspired you to read this book. Then, indicate what you hope to accomplish in it. Put it in an envelope, seal it, and tuck it away in a safe place.

CHAPTER THREE:
Ingredients That Don't Mix: What Gets in the Way

Is there only one person with whom you *really* wish to make contact? If you are excluding the possibility of anyone else coming through, this could severely limit the scope of your learning. Often the person you most want to contact will not be the first to arrive of whom you are aware. Try to become comfortable as you go along with the idea that if some information is coming through there is a reason for it. So be careful not to limit yourself in this process by being willing to receive only those whom you want to contact and hearing only what you want to hear.

I am asked frequently during a session why some other person in the family didn't show up? My answer is that if they didn't show up it might be that you have some preconceived ideas of *how* they are to show up. This happens mostly in a group or seminar, rarely in a one-on-one session. It is different when the connection comes through me than when you are doing it on your own. If they don't come or haven't come after practicing the tools you will be given, it is usually because you are not ready emotionally. Sometimes, if you are not ready, the DPS can go to other people, or other family members, to make a connection. They take their cues from you.

There is a great story that I wrote about in *Second Chance* that is an example of why we can't make a connection. It was told by Dr. Phil McGraw on Oprah's show. He was speaking to a woman who lost her daughter ten years before and who was still in a state of grief and despair. I will tell it again here to give some added insight into why sometimes our loved ones don't show up. It's one of my favorites:

Everyday God gathers all of the young people, and gives them a lit candle to guide them into his garden. As they enter, His garden greets them with an array of beautiful trees, birds, soft waterfalls, and assorted fragrances of brightly colored flowers and most of all, serenity and comfort.

God would sit and admire all that played and enjoyed each other's company. This pleased him yet He was aware and remained vigilant over one young child that would never enter into His garden. One day, He approached this beloved child and told him that He noticed that he chose never to come into the garden.

He then asked him, "Is it because you do not want to?"

The child looked up at God and said, "Oh, no, I would love to come into your garden."

God then said, "So, what is the problem?"

The child replied, "I cannot find my way because my mother's tears keep putting my candle out."

If you are trying to connect or heal, particularly in relation to children, your emotions are the biggest factor that will determine the possibility of that not happening.

Conflicts

When you are trying to connect or heal an issue, if you continue to hold on to your outdated thinking, emotions, inappropriate behaviors and patterns while attempting to mix those with new concepts and tools, you are in for a rough go of it.

Issues, fears, or religious beliefs may slow your progress. You may have been conditioned to believe that God, or your Higher Source will punish you if you pursue making a connection with

one who has passed over. Such strongly felt emotions can cloud the connection. For some, trying to make contact with loved ones who have passed over will be the most difficult process they've ever attempted. For others, it will feel like going home, that is, a feeling they've known their whole lives but were not able to share or describe in words. So, you may also want to think about a time when you might have had contact by some other means—music, pets, a funny saying you used to hear, and others. We will address some of the many ways contact may have happened when we talk about "ingredients" in Chapter Six.

Once the door has been opened, and you know you have been given a message or felt the presence of a loved one, you will always want more. This, however, may not be possible. You may have to let go and let them move on. Your issues are for *you* to heal.

Because you and the DPs are on different frequencies, you and they must learn to make adjustments. You must raise your frequency, and they must lower theirs for communication to take place. Thought is a much quicker way of communicating than movement in the physical

Issues, fears, or religious beliefs may slow your progress.

body—thought to thought communication is very fast. You may have the experience of performing routine activities, and daydreaming at the same time, when something or someone flashes into your thoughts. As quickly as it comes, if you are not aware, the image or sensation may slip away. It is in this state of mind that inspirations, ideas, and contact with the *spirit world* take place. So, stay open, because if you are fearful and closed up,

33

you run the risk of missing a vital passageway and the route to those who have passed over. What happens with most people is that the moment they know that they have had communication; the right brain gets pushed aside by the left brain, which rushes in to discredit the message. Logic has you say, "Nothing happened. I made it up."

Another caution is that you must be very careful about who you choose to tell about your new practice. They might have issues that will create blocks for you. So, whom do you tell? The answer could be maybe no one—especially not at first. I believe, having learned it somewhat painfully, that you cannot share the wishes of your heart or the goals of your mind with everybody. Even those closest to you may feel threatened or amused, or simply be unable to accept any of this. Some truly mean well; for others, what you are doing comes too close to their own fears of death. They may very well say to you something like, "You are only doing this because you can't accept the death of so and so, and you want to believe they didn't really die." Sometimes, your "secret heart" must be kept "close to the chest." If you do find supportive listeners, however, treasure them.

> **The lack of patience can also be a block to moving forward in your work on connections.**

The lack of patience can also be a block to moving forward in your work on connections. We live in a fast food society, and are conditioned to getting what we want now. If we don't learn to have patience with ourselves while developing our abilities to connect, we will most likely become frustrated and abandon our efforts. Ultimately *fast foods*—spiritual band-aids—do not nourish the soul nor help with its healing. We have become very spoiled wanting and, most of the time, expecting instant results. If you expect to connect "instantly," you are in for a rude awakening. This doesn't rule out the possibility that you may have an immediate feeling or

We are working on forgiveness— not just theirs, but yours . . .

some sensation of a presence. But, in my experience, connection usually requires more time than we think. Patience is essential.

You need to discover what might hinder you in unlocking your hidden potential to connect with a loved one. Ask yourself some questions. Were you the caretaker for him or her and have some leftover anger about that? Were you thrown into a role in the family you did not want to take on? Might some unresolved issue that you have be getting in your way? Are you resisting practicing forgiveness? Was the loved one with whom you want to connect the victim of a violent death, murder, or did he or she commit suicide? Are you dealing with some guilt or anger about that death that is holding you back? Were you hurt by the one you are attempting to contact, and have some deep-seated feelings about him or her that you now want to resolve? Perhaps you were adopted and your biological parent has passed over. In your desire to contact him or her, is there any anger getting in your way? It is critical that you address your anger before you try to make contact. Otherwise, it might not happen. We are working on forgiveness—not just theirs, but yours—so it is important to recognize who is really holding on to the negative emotions.

Sometimes a block can be created if the loved one is a parent who seemed to have favorites and you don't perceive yourself to

have been one of them. Or, there can be some ongoing sibling rivalry that is getting in your way. Maybe for some reason you were labeled the "outcast," a label still fueling emotions that might also hinder you. Perhaps you have lost a child and are passionate about finding out if he or she is okay, or you might want to send a message that conveys how much you love and miss that child. This need may give off an energy which, if too intense, can present a block to connection. You may have distanced yourself from the rest of the family, become estranged from them, but now you may want to have some kind of reconciliation with them. There are many reasons that can cause us to have a feeling of disconnection with the person we want to contact. It is important to examine the relationship we had with that person as well as the reason we might be feeling some angst about a connection. A good deal of the time I find that people are anxious to connect out of a sense of guilt. Guilt is not a good conductor—love is.

For those of you who have lost children, you must know that in spirit they are still hugging you. They want you to know they are well now and that they still love you very much. They don't need you to "make it better" for them anymore. They *are* better. Connections with children who have passed over can be the most difficult ones to make because of the emotions of the adult involved. In such a situation, being patient is critical. There may be times when you will want to toss your cookbook across the floor. Don't. Remember instead that children and animals are the quickest to recognize connections from the DPs. If you have children, listen to *them*. They are most receptive to receiving a message from another child who has passed over. If they make the contact, in spite of all your diligent efforts, don't be resentful—be grateful that they could when you could not.

Blocks caused from sudden loss

The following are some blocks that may get in the way of our connecting that we have no control over. These can be challenging contacts to make.

✻ **Suicide** For the living, the deep pain of losing someone from suicide can be incomprehensible. For those who have taken their own lives, what we usually don't realize is that the shock to them is also real. Death provides no escape for them. DPs who have committed suicide discover a hard-core truth: *you cannot kill yourself.* Their essence, state of mind, and consciousness remain, with full knowledge of why they took their lives in the first place. Suicide will not solve any problems; it only eliminates the body as a place in which to work them out. The concept of curtailing one's own life span "before the allotted time" is profound. There is a blueprint. Some DPs have said that drug abuse also shortens a life span and does not follow that blueprint. However the life span is altered, it can result in a great deal of mental and physical pain for the living. The DP's actions will be put into balance, and they are being healed. So, be aware that making contact with a DP who has taken his or her own life is among the most deeply moving of all made. One of the key elements of processing a suicide is getting beyond the "why" it happened. Just trust the connection. Judy Collins once said something to the effect that when there is a death in the family there is a skeleton in the closet and when there is a suicide there is a skeleton in everyone's closet.

A great resource for support is *The American Foundation for Suicide Prevention.* http://www.afsp.org

❋ **Murder** When a loved one has met death as the result of murder the effect can also be, like suicide, deeply traumatic. But, hard as it is to realize, the DPs are not physically connected to how they exited, yet often they will make contact because they know the living need some sign that they are okay. Perhaps they will come to give us a *spiritual hug,* and open our eyes to the possibility of a richer life—if we find ways to move on. When something happens to us physically we retain the memory, not the pain. When someone passes from an act of violence, they do not continue to experience the means by which they were killed *or* the pain. The *physicality* of it all has passed too. It is the same for suicide cases. For these loved ones, our prayers are really significant for them, *and* for those who are left.

❋ **Accidental deaths** elicit much of the same responses as those discussed above. In all such sudden losses, blocks are often generated out of the greatest need to understand. The grieving process is long and necessary. Making contact with a loved one in *spirit* will not end the grief, but it may ease some of the anguish and let the healing begin.

I encourage you to take an honest look at the relationships you had with the DPs you want to contact, and what effects they had on you. If you feel blocked and frustrated, it is important to understand why. I hope that you will discover through this book that the DPs—the speakers in spirit—communicate in a multitude of ways of which most of us are unaware. By creating a cookbook with you as the chef in charge, you get to decide how to prepare your own ingredients for your meals—that is to say, prepare yourself for your communications.

As a final note on removing a block, I urge you to keep in mind that the DPs do not need or want you to let their deaths take over your life. What they do need from you are your prayers, something so often forgotten or ignored. When you offer prayers—words and thoughts—for someone else, living or dead, you are giving that person and all his or her circumstances to God, or a Higher Source. Words and thoughts are energy. You need not be in close proximity to send "prayer energy" to someone. Please, then, believe in the power that prayer has even over what is, conceptually, the longest possible distance for us—from this life to the next. I don't believe we can erase all that pains us about a loss, but we can move to a place that takes us out of our feeling of *victimization* surrounding that loss.

RECIPE CARD:

 List what blocks—emotions, resistances, issues, negative voices—might get in your way.

 Are you open to making changes?

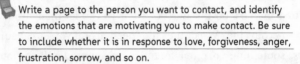 Write a page to the person you want to contact, and identify the emotions that are motivating you to make contact. Be sure to include whether it is in response to love, forgiveness, anger, frustration, sorrow, and so on.

Commitment to "Cooking": The Importance of Intention

Understanding why are you doing this

One of the most important things to understand as you begin this journey of connection is that you have to be clear about *why* you are doing this. Again, I provide you with some important questions to ask yourselves. What is your intention for your journey? What is the course of action you intend to follow? What is your purpose for making contact? You should have some idea by now about why you want to connect, but before you take the step of learning how to go about it you must clarify your intention to yourself, and resolve to be firm in your commitment to stay the course. Working this learning process consists of an ongoing practice of reevaluating many parts of your life. As I keep reminding you, this is not *just* about making a connection with a loved one who has passed over, it is also about your soul's program. One of the elements of your success is your consistency and dedication to your practice. Yes, you will experience mental fatigue, and at times you might feel out of sorts. But, I urge you not to let this discourage you. Eventually you will get stronger. Patience is the key.

To return to our cookbook language, do you want to continue eating "frozen dinners" or would you like to prepare the finest meals you can? Many people who go to cooking schools do not go to work directly (or ever) in fine restaurants. Everyone in the "cooking business" has experienced, at one time or another, some loss and made some changes before or even after their success. You may find along the way that you have to undergo some loss yourself to receive a gain. As you move forward in your commitment, the important thing is to keep at it. The longer and more consistent you are in the practice of creating your own recipes for connection, the more noticeable the results will become. So dig deep and embrace whatever you may discover and soon you will realize that you have given yourself the opportunity to heal, honor, explore, and address all your relationships—living or dead. You will come to a greater understanding of the choices you have made in your life, and move on to another level of your soul's program.

Clarity of intention will illuminate your passageway to connection. Otherwise you may wind up getting muddled messages that can only frustrate you. Also, if you make a commitment to this practice, and then take no action at all to anchor that commitment, the process will falter, and you will remain in the pain you find yourself in now. If you are not "checking-in" with yourself daily throughout this work, then you will not know how you feel or what is occurring in and around you. Doubt will then creep in and become a barrier to your progress. You have an opportunity now to create more than just a "sandwich and chips" meal for yourself; you are heading toward creating a banquet. Take hold of that opportunity now. You must be honest with yourself about whether or not this is what you really want to do, or just something you heard about that sounds interesting. If you feel strongly that doing this is right for you, then it is time to surrender all resistance to the process.

Facing solitude

If solitude is difficult for you, you may want to take some time to think about whether you are ready for this kind of practice. Solitude is a fundamental part of the ingredients

Patience is the key.

you will be learning to create. It is okay to be uneasy with the thought of being alone, as long as you are willing to give it a try. I once heard someone say, "Until we experience the freedom of solitude, we cannot connect authentically," and that is what we want to reach for—authentic connection. One of our major efforts is to lose our "false selves" in order to connect to those we love both here and in the spirit world. As you become more and more comfortable with the self you are rediscovering, you will find that others will notice the change in you. Do you have the sense of self-worth to stay with your practice, or will you abandon it for fear of what others think? If you think this might be a problem for you, it would be good to identify those

. . . *it is okay to seek support.*

who can become blocks to your progress, and back away from them for the next few weeks. Let us look at the possible blocks we have identified, especially those to whom we have become quite attached. It is important to understand that as we begin to challenge those blocks, our egos can become very protective of us and want to demonstrate that even more powerfully than they did before. It is paramount that during these times not to give in to those blocks and stop the work. When we are stretching the most in our growth are the times when we will hear our inner voices. Those of fear and ego will be loud, screaming negative directions and doubt. The voice of faith, however, will say quietly, "Go for it. You will have everything you need." That is the voice I hope you choose to follow.

Take a look at your record of past commitments and ask yourself some questions. Have you followed through or have you

usually abandoned your commitments? Are you conditioned to following through with what you start? Or, even when you have the best intentions of not doing so, do you give up? When you need support, will you ask for it? And, it is okay to seek support. Do you know where to go for positive support? Where do your patterns of behavior around commitment come from? Answering these will go a long way toward clarifying your intentions and will make the work of getting connected solid.

Now let us bring some clarity around what we think about intention and commitment.

Intention

- What is your definition of intention?
- What does it mean to "set" an intention?
- Name one intention you have set in the past that has come to fruition. What do you think made that happen?
- What did you do to make sure this intention would be successful?
- Name one intention you set in the past that didn't come to fruition. What happened?
- Who is the DP you are intending to contact now? What is the intention of that connection?
- How will you set that intention?

Commitment

- What is your definition of commitment? What does it mean to you to make a commitment?

What is one commitment in which you have followed through? What did you do to assure the follow through?

Why do you believe you kept your commitment?

Name one commitment you made in which you didn't follow through. How did that feel?

What commitment are you making now? Why is this commitment important to you?

What do you plan to achieve by making this commitment?

Basic Principles

What are the basic principles you live by?

Why are they important to you?

How do you think you will apply them to the work before you?

Commitments are important, but most important are those we make to ourselves, and if we break them, most of the time we are the only ones who know. Nonetheless, breaking a commitment chips away at our sense of self-worth. As we set an intention to give any course of action our best effort, it is vital to the process that we establish a contract with ourselves at the onset. Most intentions fail when we don't create a "check and balance" system to assist us in maintaining our integrity, commitments, and a clear vision of what we are doing. If we find ourselves "off-course," we can come back to our commitment and can re-ignite our energy to go forward. Following is a contract that I believe will support you in this process of expanding your consciousness. When you are

45

feeling blocked, frustrated, or having a sense of "what's the use," I recommend you come back and revisit your contract.

Commitment and Intention Contract

I, _____, am fully conscious of the commitment I am making herein to make contact with a loved one who has passed over, and my intention is for the highest and greatest good for the both of us. I commit to a daily practice of the ingredients/tools I am about to be given, and give myself over wholly to executing them to the best of my ability.

I understand that the practice of these tools may give rise to emotions and issues that I have to this point kept hidden, and will direct my best efforts toward addressing and healing those "blocks" in order to create a connection of the purest kind.

I embrace the fact that this journey is really about my soul's program. The resolutions I receive from this practice and the connections I may make are for the continuing growth of my soul's journey.

_____ (name)

_____ (date)

RECIPE CARD:

 Check your intentions about connecting to a loved one who has passed over.

 Make a commitment to "check in" with yourself daily. Perhaps this is a good time to review your notes you have made in your journals.

 Make a commitment also to exercising the best self-care you can while on this course of expansion.

Recipes for Success
— Harnessing Your Abilities

Recipe for Adventure: Embracing the Explorer in You

The more trusting you are,
the more you will trust the explorer in you.

To begin with let us think about what we have been told, read, seen, or done to help us explore making connections with loved ones who have passed over. What have you heard? What experience have you had that can reveal to what degree there is an explorer in you? Take a moment to think about what that experience did for you. Have you been curious enough about connecting to seek out a workshop, or professional presenter? To look at it another way, have you been curious *and* at the same time fearful of seeking these out, anxious that some friend or family member would find out and chastise you? Has it been a bit scary thinking about what might happen, or what you might discover along the way?

An explorer, by definition, is someone who travels into unknown regions, who seeks adventure and enjoys taking risks. Maybe you don't think that doing any of this is in your nature, that it is too great a challenge; or, maybe you are someone who is quite comfortable with stepping out into the unknown. I hope that if you are one who has been conditioned to resist taking risks and exploring, you will stretch yourself enough to delve into a realm that has until now been uncomfortable for you. There is nothing more exciting than discovering something new, some new situation, place, or some new understanding of yourself that sparks a sense of expanded reality within you and offers you an amplified existence. Connecting with an inner source that says to *go for it* is a connection that often has given me the fuel to continue when I have wanted to give up. There is nothing like it. When that voice speaks, listen. Ninety-nine percent of the time that inner voice will never lead us into harm's way. When we find ourselves asking, "Is this all there is?" is the point in our lives when what lies at the core of our beings can support the choice to investigate. If you believe you can, *you can!*

The most common illusion about how the dead folks communicate is that they just "show up." This can happen, but it is the least likely kind of manifestation. When you start listing the ways they can show up, as you will learn, they can show up often when we are doing non-linear things—household chores, showering, music, driving, and so on. You will explore all the ways I give you when your are learning the tools, which I call *Ingredients* in Chapter Six. When they do show up—you feel like you had a communication—but if you're questioning *if* it was a communication, you might want to pay attention to the time and the date that this happens because it may have significance. Does it validate anyone in the family that has passed over? Does the time have numerical value for that loved one? Did they pass at this time, or was it a date to remember like a birth date or a celebration? Does it signify a date that is important concerning this loved one? Does a certain piece of music have any connection to the loved one?

I have a friend whose brother passed over last year. His sister-in-law recently called to talk about missing him and shared this story:

> *Ninety-nine percent of the time that inner voice will never lead us into harm's way.*

The other day, Shelby [his granddaughter] and I were out doing some things and she was talking continuously about Papa Bob and how she missed him. But, she said, that she knew he was always around and still talked to her. We were at the mall and in different stores throughout the day, and everywhere we went the song he loved was playing. Even as we got in the car and were leaving, the song was on the radio. Now I know this was his favorite song and it was played at his funeral. Could it be that he was really connecting with us? My friend said to her, "Well, duh? If you don't think he was contacting you, then you don't believe in life-after-death. He was letting you and Shelby know that he was still around."

Don't discredit the way you can be contacted. Be open to new ways of communication.

The DPs are aware that a sudden appearance might terrify the living. It is also the most difficult method for them. Their primary desire, as I have said, is to let you know that they are fine, not dead, and that they will be with you when your time comes. They don't usually need to say or do more, although you may want more. Your loved one is able to hear you, and you can connect with him or her on your own, but you must remember that communication with a person in "spirit" is different from ordinary communication in method and components. In order for satisfactory communication to happen, you will need to work on developing some new skills to learn how to use new tools and ingredients. That is why you have come to this point in your soul's program—you want to know how. It is time for you to step out and become the adventurer. Remember, the DPs are ready, willing, and very able to communicate. It's up to you to learn the ingredients that will enhance your ability to do so.

This course of study is about learning the art of intuitive "inner listening."

Now, since you have chosen to pursue making connections on your own, I want to say that this journey is about unlearning the indiscriminate dependence on "critical and practical thinking." This course of study is about learning the art of intuitive "inner listening." We must move away from the overly stressed need for analysis, and move into a place of trust. The work we are going to do is about moving into the domain of our "sixth sense," because when we become comfortable with our sixth sense, all our other senses are heightened and combined. Our sixth sense connects all the other senses. We must move beyond the need to have things come to us in a dramatic way and learn to listen to the subtle ways our "intuitive psyche" speaks. Some examples of tuning into that intuition are thinking something is going to happen before it does, knowing who is calling on the phone before you pick up, or someone saying something at the same time you are thinking it. I put a huge premium on the "little signals" we get all the time.

If you can resolve those doubts and fears with which you have been inculcated, you will come to believe that you *can* do this. You'll be preparing yourself to hear whatever messages the DPs need to send, even if they bring up issues or thoughts that might be disturbing to you. These are disturbing only because you hang onto some energy around an issue that hasn't found understanding and resolution yet. Such disturbances are caused sometimes by your inability to find forgiveness in yourself, others present, or those who have passed on. Remember, DPs don't carry resentment, fear, or anger. They have moved on. Most are in a state of joy and compassion.

Having trust is a key element in what we are trying to do here. Trusting is the way to start eliminating your fear and you may find that even when you don't think so, you may very well be connecting. It is as if our loved ones are just a phone call away—unless the signal is interrupted. There is no perfect process in this case, however, honesty is the key to pushing on. Getting caught up in the notion of perfection can only lead to procrastination and paralysis. Other than the Divine God, no one has all

Acknowledge your courage before you go any further.

the answers: making a connection, then, is about moving on to another level, and you will find as I do that everything happens for a reason.

As we begin, give yourself a pat on the back because you are about to enter a realm of exploration that stirs most people's greatest fears and doubts—life after death. Although you may have attended a session or a workshop with a professional like me, you are now choosing to believe that there is some part of "connecting" that you can learn to do on your own. Kudos to you, my friend! You will learn to listen with more intent and conscious awareness of what your feelings, thoughts, and inner voices have been trying to convey for a long time. I think you will find that like most fears met head-on, they are not as fearful as you thought. Acknowledge your courage before you go any further. Throughout this work, you will come to understand that the DPs want to make contact with those who remain alive, and that you now have opportunity to increase the chances of making those contacts. You will also realize—in regard to whatever it is you have been unable to forgive, forget, or let go of—a connection to a loved one who has passed over can bring healing messages for all of your relationships. The DPs glory in the spirit of courage in the afterlife. They would like you to find that courage now. This is your chance to learn how to tune into the vibrations or frequencies of a specific loved one in order to receive the information they are trying to bring you. I have been doing this for others for years and I, in turn, have felt the healing in my soul. Now, it is your turn!

As we progress deeper into this study, I would like to share with you the beliefs I carry as I do my work. Maybe you can embrace some of these for yourself as you step out to connect with your spiritual adventurer.

- There is a Higher Power.
- Life is a series of relationships.
- Death is a continuation of many of those relationships.
- Relationship problems should be worked out now because they don't go away, and it is a lot harder working them out later. Many of us don't work out the problems, for so many different reasons, and are left with grief, guilt, or anger when the other person passes on.
- You are able to work out your problems with the loved one even after they have passed over.
- You'll receive information from the DPs but not instructions: guidance from them—yes, decisions—no. They will not interfere with your path.

🥄 I believe I have been given a gift, and the Higher Power intends that I share it with others.

You may have fears around how you might respond when someone shows up that you are not expecting. As the explorer, you have to learn to work with that manifestation constructively rather than destructively. Most importantly, you will have to learn not to analyze, but just accept what is coming through to you. The gift in all of this work is that you are given the opportunity to assess your abilities: those you have and those you need to hone.

Staying anchored to the explorer in you opens the door to new thinking . . .

What is before you is the prospect of creating a new viewpoint around how you perceive things. Staying anchored to the explorer in you opens the door to new thinking, and trying out the ingredients and tools you are learning about. It opens you to a whole new world of experiences in your life. Maybe you already consider yourself an explorer. What in you has allowed you to feel that kind of self-validation? Was it something you were taught, or something you have uncovered on your own? Is there some practice you have already discovered that has instilled that quality in you? If so, we certainly don't want to discard it if it is working, we want to expand it. Just as with those invaluable tips that help make our recipes successful—spiritual exercises, creative expressions, and daily rituals—we want to build onto what we already know and perhaps, if we can, add a new insight or two. If you don't know it by now, you are about to understand more deeply that your essential nature is spirit, and that it knows no boundaries. This practice is about opening up and going deeper, and that doing so takes the kind of courage that both comes from and produces an increased sense of self-worth.

As you have probably begun to realize, the real effort for us is to step outside the conditioning that we are all subject to that prevents and inhibits our growth. It is now time to get beyond those boundaries. Life just doesn't happen to you—you are your life! So, can you make a commitment to the adventure of making your life special to you? What you came here seeking can lead you to much more than you ever realized. What I am asking you to do is to become engaged in your own life. Does that scare you? How often have you been told that you could not do something? And, how often have you given into that statement and really believed that you could not do it? How did it make you feel? Not very capable, I would imagine. To become the explorer, and set yourself on a course for an extraordinary adventure, you have to take risks. It is important to examine what you were told growing up about breaking conventions, doing something different, or exploring the unknown. Are you willing to make changes in your beliefs, routines, patterns, and thinking in order to have a more conscious and rewarding existence? Then, let's start right now by casting some light on what may have had an influence on your ability to be or not to be the explorer. Answer the following questions as honestly as you can, and then take some time to review your answers. It is important to evaluate how comfortable you are with exploring. You want to examine those times when you have been willing to take the risk of exploring, and if you were not, why you were resistant to it. Looking at how you were conditioned when you were growing up around being the adventurer can be quite revealing as you move forward.

The Explorer:

- Were you encouraged to take risks when you were growing up?
- What games did you play as a child?
- How often did you imagine yourself on an adventure?
- How often did you take an adventure and what/where was it?
- What is one adventure you have always wanted to take, but have not? What is one step you can take now to start that happening?
- Do you feel you live within conventional norms or outside them today?
- What do you need to bring more awareness to in your life?
- On a scale of 1-10, where do you feel your self-esteem and self-acceptance lies?
- On a scale of 1-10, where is your ability to take risks?
- Name one person that you admire as an explorer in life.

Now, take a breath and inhale what you have discovered about yourself in the questions above. The time has come to take the next step in stretching toward the explorer that you will become.

RECIPE CARD:

 Commit to taking a "new" step outside your comfort zone once a week.

 Think of something you have wanted to do, and do it! Are you experiencing resistance, or other emotions? What immediately comes up for you? Were you successful? Write it down.

 In your journal write about the experience you hope to have by learning to expand your consciousness and your ability to connect.

The Main "Ingredients": Choosing and Working with Your Tools

You can cook too!

Any great recipe for what you want to prepare starts with the best ingredients—*tools*—you can gather for the most successful outcome possible. So it is with connecting. Understanding the ingredients, what tools are available, can greatly enhance your practice and ability to make those desired connections to loved ones. So, after examining why you want to "cook"—*connect*— and what issues you are bringing to the "table," you have come to an understanding of your intention to uncover, as much as is possible for now, what might get in your way. Now, you are ready to begin your adventure. It is time to step into the energy of the *explorer*.

To begin with, you must let your loved ones know that you want to reach them, and when you'll be expecting their contact—a bit like planning a meal and deciding who will join you at the table. So, *make an appointment with them.* When it comes time for you to launch yourself as "chef," choose a time when you're not likely to be disturbed or feeling anxious about having to do other things. Don't, for example, make an appointment for 5:30 on Tuesday if you know your children, spouse, or roommates will be around. For this practice, I've found that early mornings or late evenings are usually best. And remember, whatever tool you may choose to enhance your ability to connect, it must be practiced in a space whose atmosphere is sacred to you and protects your privacy.

You can decide on how much time you will need for accomplishing your goals for this project. Be sure to set yourself up for success, I have found that committing to a period of seven to eight weeks works well. Don't start when you know you will be on a business trip or flying to your best friend's wedding in Boise the week after next. When you've decided on a time, repeat your commitment once or twice, either aloud or to yourself: "Monday morning, at 7 a.m., I'll be open to receiving communications from ——." You can ask for a specific person if you like, but be prepared for others who may also show up. They can show up in any of the ingredients—tools—I am offering here. All of the tools you are about to learn how to use, may serve to ignite your memories by heightening and extending your senses. Also, be aware that when you are practicing making a connection, contact doesn't always happen immediately. More commonly, you will recognize or receive a connection within the next day or two, and when you least expect it. Now, let us don our aprons and step into the kitchen.

You can ask for a specific person if you like, but be prepared for others who may also show up.

Ingredient #1: Meditation

Meditation is one of the greatest tools one can use to open the doors of perception and connection. Here is a meditation practice to get you started. At some point before the designated time set to start your practice, you will have found a place or created one in which you will be comfortable, relaxed, and uninterrupted for whatever period of time you have set aside. This place will be your "kitchen" for the next seven or eight weeks. As you go along, or immediately afterwards, it is a good idea to jot down in your journal what has come to you during this time so that you may review it now or refer to it later. If random thoughts occur during your meditation, acknowledge them and let them go. Take note: don't think too much, just flow with the adventure. It is time to begin:

Making initial contact

1. Several minutes before your appointed time to begin, take the phone off the hook, go to your chosen location, and try to prepare your mind. Make sure you are comfortable, no binding clothing, stomach neither too full nor too empty, and allow your body to relax. Close your eyes and try to empty your mind, while attempting to tune into your *inner ear*. Imagine a beautiful glowing white light beginning to envelope your body, mind, and spirit.

2. Once you feel a sense of safety and protection from the surrounding light, begin to breathe deeply from your diaphragm, noticing the air as it passes in and out of your nostrils/mouth.

3. Request permission of God, Higher Power, or whomever you look to as your Greater Source, to allow your loved ones to come through and express your gratitude to that entity for this special moment. Then, seal the light and the permission with a prayer, in whatever words you choose, directed to whomever will give you peace of mind and the understanding that whatever happens will be for the highest good.

4. Now take a moment with each name you wish to contact. Say that name out loud a few times and feel the vibration, assume you have gotten their attention, even if you have no indication of this.

5. In your own words, simply ask them to also reveal in some way if they have ever tried to contact you. Ask if you can be reminded of this contact experience.

6. Now ask if you can be shown details of this through mental picturing. The idea here is to try to recognize moments in the past when a DP has tried to contact you; it will help you recognize those contacts more readily in the future.

7. Ask if you can receive a message right now. Ask, "Can I receive contact today?" Then wait for an inner answer. Again write down whatever comes, even if you catch yourself saying, "I'm just making this up."

8. When you feel it is time to "return," give thanks for what you have received. Then, in your journal, begin describing everything you received under each name, no matter how random it may seem. Contact with DPs is very much like one of those 3-D pictures that can look like chaos up close, but quite different when seen from a distance. Allow your "seeing" to go deeper, and a larger picture or subject may be revealed. So don't discount anything that arrives. Just write down whatever comes to you as if you were an impartial observer.

Allow your "seeing" to go deeper, and a larger picture or subject may be revealed.

The point of this meditation is to jog your subconscious memory, not only for specific instances of contact, but also to prompt you to recall what a forgotten or unperceived contact felt like so that you may recognize such instances of contact in the future. After doing this a few times, you will have already memorized the steps to this meditation procedure.

A guided meditation

The following is a meditation I use in groups that has produced some wonderful connections for the participants. Read this through first, and memorize the process so you can practice it without having to look back at the page. Once you have completed it, it will become an automatic tool that can be used over and over. Start by taking deep breaths, remembering that the breath opens the door to the "mystery":

As you become more relaxed, feel yourself being lifted gently upward as if in a balloon of light, leaving your daily cares and worries behind. You are now being lifted toward a door above you that opens as you approach, and allows you to pass through into a beautiful field of flowers. You feel warm and protected and loved.

As you move through the field, you see a gazebo with a bench ahead of you. Someone is waiting for you on the bench. You may or may not see the person clearly, but you move toward the bench and sit down next to him or her. You feel his or her love touching you. Even if you don't see or feel the person, you know somehow he or she is near. You hear a *word* with your inner ear. You may not know immediately what it means, but you know that later you will understand. If you can see the other person, look into his or her eyes. If you hear a familiar voice, remain silent and listen. If you feel a touch, be still. You'll know when your time is over. I can't explain how; you just will. At that moment, silently tell yourself and

> **You may not know immediately what it means, but you know that later you will understand.**

your loved one that it is time to go. As you leave the bench, you'll sense that you are once more alone. As you walk back through the field and reenter your balloon of light, you will feel comforted, and you will know that you can return to this special place again and again.

As you are lowered gently, securely, back through the door, the light will begin to fade and you will feel yourself returning to your normal state of consciousness. You may not be certain of exactly what has happened, but you'll feel relaxed, secure, and loved in a unique way.

Cling to those feelings for a moment. This is a special moment that may very well remain imprinted in your mind.

Now, begin to write down what you experienced in your journal.

Another note on meditation: there are a myriad of ways to meditate. The one above is an initial way for you to make contact, but it is certainly not the *only* way to meditate. For many of us, the notion of sitting in meditation brings to mind mental images of sitting in a lotus position and repeating the mantra, *ohm,* in a low, drawn out tone. While this may work for some, we are attempting a different kind of connection here. Meditating to "let go to our inner ear" can be practiced in other ways. I will talk about these later in this chapter.

> **Do not allow the "editor" and "critic" voice—your mind's censor—to grab hold of you.**

Ingredient #2: Journaling Your Meditation Experience

Immediately after your meditation, or the practice of any "ingredient," you will want to write down everything you saw or felt, no matter how little or how much. Even if it seems like very little to you at first, you'll be empowering your ongoing process by writing. Do not allow the "editor" and "critic" voice—your mind's censor—to grab hold of you. Write down anything and everything, whether it makes sense to you at the moment or not, whether it seems significant or not. This information will continue to become clear as you spend time with it, and the only way you can do that is to write it down and have it at hand. Being as thorough as you possibly can about this is an indication of your respect and sincerity. It is not a trivial parlor game, nor should the reason for contact be merely the novelty of the contact itself. The idea is to

> **There is something that happens when you are in the physical act of writing . . .**

receive guidance and instruction around the unfolding of your soul's program—-your recipes for connection. The DPs are out of the *game* here on earth, but they can, and want to coach you from the sidelines. You are still in the kitchen of life, so to speak, and need to focus on your personal journey. Review your notes periodically to keep matters fresh in your mind and to reinforce the process.

Ingredient #3: Journals and Journaling

A journal is a personal place of expression for all of us. It is an important tool for unearthing what lays beneath in our conscious mind, that is, our inner voice. We will use journals for many of the activities and practices we are attempting to learn about here.

Honesty while journaling is key to unlocking whatever it is you are seeking along this journey. It is paramount, then, that you keep your journals in a safe place, one that cannot be violated and exposed. If they are not secured, you will find yourself writing in a restrictive mindset causing you to be hesitant and fearful. It can prevent you from accomplishing your evolution. So, keep your journal private—it is *your* soul's diary.

If you are one of those people who does everything on a computer, and would rather type in journal entries instead of writing them down by hand, I say to you emphatically, *please resist the impulse to type!* Pick up a pen or pencil instead. Part of the process of journaling, or any review of your experiences with the subconscious for that matter, is helped by the slower pace and the deliberate formation of thought into written ideas letter by letter, word by word—*by hand.* Something happens between the lines when you write on paper: as the mind is preoccupied for a moment with writing one thought, it is out of the way enough for a second thought to occur in a natural progression. Thus, the slower pace of writing by hand aids the deepening of what is revealed. There is something that happens when you are in the physical act of writing, more recollections seem to slip through as the thoughts travel down the arm, to the hand and fingers, and out onto the paper. The natural rhythm of writing becomes a distraction to the *inner critic*. Also, it can be done in any supportive environment, not just wherever a computer happens to be connected.

I am sure there are those who will say they can do this perfectly well while typing. Well, more power to you! I believe, however, that you will be cheating yourself. I have always found that the tactile scrape of pencil lead, or the scratch of the pen point, on paper fiber becomes a resonant counterpoint to a good flow of ideas. The right and left-brain harmonize with the hand, if only for a moment, and this is less likely to happen typing in front of a screen. Something magical can happen when it comes out of the body/mind/spirit collaboration: down the

Give yourself permission to create.

arm, through the hand and writing utensil, and onto the paper. You might just surprise yourself if you write by hand! So, my vote is for doing your journaling with pen/pencil and paper.

Creating those special journals
Basic Journal Decoration:
A minimal requirement for the
"you've-got-to-be-kidding-me" crowd.

Set the timer for 30 minutes, no interruptions. Before hand, get out or purchase some colorful pens, watercolors, inks, stickers, or crayons. (Don't worry about the expense; you will be using these implements again and again throughout your practice.) Now, sit down for this time period and be willing to play. Squiggle and doodle on your journal cover. Draw symbols, or else start with the borders, drawing shapes, outlines, and patterns—anything that comes to mind that pleases you.

This is an exercise in which there is no right or wrong, no grade, or expectation. The whole idea is to let your free-associating artistic self emerge. Get "dreamy" and let your ideas flow into unselfconscious design fun! If you find your mind is taking you back to some thoughts of the classroom with this exercise: *snap out of it!* I mean actually snap your fingers in front of your face a few times, and then make a loud goofy noise that you could never do in a classroom and go back to decorating. Give yourself permission to create. Whatever you draw, a favorite animal, stars and moons in the night sky, an abstract design, or a doodle, is all wonderful because it is yours.

Advanced Journal Decoration:
A more committed project for the adventurous and artistic.

The point of this exercise is to create a cover for your journal that will remind you symbolically of the terrain you are exploring within. Open up your connection to your *inner* self by covering the journal with images that call out to you. Before you start doing this journal cover, find some old magazines, preferably ones with great photographs or text you can cut out and use—garden and travel types are excellent. Scan them quickly for images that strike you as beautiful, meaningful, or powerful in some way. Don't try to read anything, but if a title or a few lines of text do jump out at you, take note. We are looking for imagery and statements that pull at your heart. When something grabs your attention, cut it out. Keep an envelope of these images until you have enough to cover the journal you plan to work on.

In her book, *The Artist's Way,* Julia Cameron calls this the "image well." Her point is that by viewing and immersing ourselves in beautiful imagery, we fill the well of our artistic creativity so that we may draw ideas and inspiration from it later. I would add that it recharges the "batteries" of the subconscious. Once you have your envelope of delicious images, start assembling them into a collage on the journal you have chosen for them. Play with them first. See how they fit together; experiment with different combinations. When you feel you have a complete collage that expresses your desires for this journal, begin gluing them into place. The reason for doing this is to practice setting yourself up for remembering and connecting to scenes and images that will come to you during your process. Taking the time to decorate this primary tool—your journal—with personally significant imagery prepares you to enter the realm of connection. These projects will help bring the artistic parts of the brain to the fore and will help open the doors to what you are seeking.

. . . dreams are one of the easiest and commonest ways the DPs have of contacting us directly.

One of your goals in keeping a journal, whether the dream journal, meditation journal, or any other, is to recognize those signs that might include communications from loved ones who have passed. This may or may not happen right away. Just because you have a "cool" looking journal, doesn't mean your DPs will start clamoring for expression. But, if anyone is trying to reach you, your journal will help you take notice.

Ingredient #4: Exploring Your Dreams

Do you have vivid dreams and wonder if they are a true contact with a loved one? Certainly not every dream in which a DP makes an appearance means that your loved one in spirit has paid a nocturnal visit. But, equally, dreams are one of the easiest and commonest ways the DPs have of contacting us directly. Why should that be? Anyone who remembers a vivid dream will understand that most dreams have symbolic, rather than purely literal content, but, when we are sleeping, the analytical, logical part of our brains also takes a rest, allowing our creative and intuitive faculties free reign. Since, as I have explained, it is with the intuitive part of our brain in which we make contact with those who've passed over, it is during sleep that we are most receptive to receiving these messages.

Dreams are also among the "safest" ways the DPs have of connecting with us. Even people, who are skeptical of the possibility that we can communicate with departed loved ones, seem relatively comfortable dreaming about the dead. Undoubtedly, that's because they use the dream itself to rationalize the experience, rather than having to accept the fact that they were actually *contacted* by a loved one in spirit. Among the most frequently reported dream experiences are those in which a loved one will say that he or she is "not dead," or that they are happy, healthy, and having a good time. That is, after all, the primary message the DPs need to send. As I have said, it is their job to let us know that they are still present, well, and not "dead" at all in the conventional sense of the word. Isn't that what we want to be reassured about?

So, if you awaken from your dream feeling peaceful and

enveloped by intense feelings of love, you have, most likely, experienced a contact with the world of spirit. Trust it. I urge you to write it down as soon as you awaken because the memory, like the memory of all dreams, will be fleeting, and if you don't write it down you will not be able to retain it. But just as you can train yourself, through meditation and practice, to make yourself more available to receiving messages, you can also train yourself to have greater access to your dream experiences. You might, for example, practice a meditation just before going to bed, and issue an invitation to your loved one to make contact while you are asleep. You might give yourself the suggestion that you will wake up when the contact is over so that you will remember it. You might not be successful the first time, or every time, but, as with everything else, you'll get better at it with practice and repetition. At the same time, however, I need to point out that if your dream makes you fearful or angry or stirs up other negative emotions, they are probably coming from you—from the base of your fears—because, as I have said, the dead people are *never* angry with you. They don't want to make you unhappy or uncomfortable, and they no longer harbor any ill will no matter what may have passed between you while they were alive.

Some dreams people experence are:

✻ **Advisory Dreams** It is amazing how advice that we refused to accept from people while they were still alive becomes something we frequently ask for when they pass over. Often, what is asked for is something they cannot give. It is your life and your responsibility to make the choices.

✳ **Precognitive Dreams** These dreams, most often, bring contact and insight prior to something happening. The soul always knows when something is going to happen, and will make every effort to give us a message. The soul is a work in progress, so it is continually trying to process what it is experiencing, for its own growth and ours. Contact dreams with loved ones that have passed over usually come right after or within the first year of the person's passing. That is sort of the rule of thumb of what happens, but for the sake of our work, you will just want to try to remember when and if you had a contact during that time. This might trigger an insight to a clue of what you might use at this time that will enhance connection. You can receive clarity, understanding, and guidance if you learn to pay attention to your dreams. One book that might assist you in a deeper understanding of dreams and their meanings is *The Woman's Book of Dreams: Dreaming as a Spiritual Practice* by Connie Cockrell Kaplan.

Morning preparation for dream recall

This is not a long, drawn-out process. It should be done as soon as you wake up, not immediately necessarily, but promptly. The whole idea is to create a bubble of clarity in your morning. Within this bubble, easily duplicated each morning without a lot of ceremonial fuss, you can grant yourself the gift of steadily improving your dream recall. Keep it simple. The more complicated you make it the easier it will become to avoid, which might prevent a

Just start writing whatever you can remember about your dreams.

helpful pattern from developing. The goal is to be able to slip from the "dream state" into the "recall state" with one foot still in the dreamtime, and then smoothly make the transition into the rest of your morning. As always, feel free to modify or adapt the meditation in any way that serves your situation.

Dream recall exercise:

Sit in the same comfortable place each day. If you can stay in bed to write, all the better.

Light a candle. Keep the ambient light low, yet bright enough to write.

Close your eyes for a moment and see yourself surrounded by a soft blue light.

Then say out loud:

"Thank you for the ability to recall all of my dreams.

"I ask that I be able to recall them fully, and that their truth and meaning be revealed to me more and more each day."

"I ask that I be fully protected and held safe throughout this process."

After journaling, pinch out the candle, give yourself a nice stretch, and slowly transition into your usual morning routine.

Your dreams will begin to reveal more and more of your subconscious to you . . .

A note on "dream journaling"

Perhaps you wake up in the morning and immediately dash to the pot of coffee and the morning paper; perhaps you have kids to bundle off to school, lunches to make, and shopping lists to write; or, perhaps you are out the door for a high-pressure meeting, and you realize you forgot to complete one important part. Whatever it may be, many morning wake-up scenes are insane whirls of activity. If this is true for you, then *dream journaling* may not be the ingredient/tool for you. The whole point of the dream journal is about taking the time to remember your dreams so you can inspect them for clues and themes later. If you wake up to chaos, there is little chance of remembering your dreams after an hour of buzzing around and zooming here and there to get yourself or someone else out the door

> **There is no need to make a great effort to think of things to say.**

The dream journal is not like any other journal you keep or may have kept in the past, so it is a good idea to have a separate journal for these notations. If you are in the habit of writing in some kind of "reflective journal," by all means continue. Yet it is best to have a separate journal for your dreams exclusively for the purpose of recalling them and eventually exploring them for clues. Buy a notebook for the job—nothing fancy. In fact, make it one that has a simple cover to allow for personalized decoration. If it does not have a blank cover, glue some pictures on the front and back to express what this specific journal might mean to you. When you are done decorating, keep it by your bed. Tie a good new pen to it with a string so you don't have to go searching for one as you are waking up. Use it every morning, no excuses, even if you don't remember anything at first. Just start writing whatever you *can* remember about your dreams. If you cannot remember anything, start writing about how you are feeling as you wake up. Often, this can open the door to what you dreamt.

The point of keeping a *dream journal* is only for assisting you in remembering your dreams more completely—not for anything else. What you may get out of this exploration of your subconscious remains to be revealed. Yet, nothing will be revealed if you cannot recall the dreams you had. About their dreams, most people say that they can remember some parts of memorable ones, but not much more. The practice of dream journaling will strengthen your ability to remember more of your dreams, as well as, more about them. Over time, you will recall with greater ease and more vivid detail. The dream journal is not a place for confessional release, nor should it be a diary for divulging in writing what cannot be spoken. Save that for your other journal. The dream journal is a place for observing your dream life, as if it were a "family recipe," and you are keeping a *recipe journal* to record any significant changes that are being made to it. Your dreams are the recipes, and like a skilled Master Chef, you are keeping detailed notes of your observations. Have your goal be simply to improve your description and recollection of your dreams. Both will improve in a short time. Your dreams will begin to reveal more and more of your subconscious to you, and perhaps a message from a passed loved one. No matter what, you will undoubtedly receive clues to some aspect of your Soul Program. "Keeping a dream journal," a teacher I had once said, "will help reveal your life's 'charismatic vocation,' or calling"—part of a Soul Program, indeed.

By keeping a dream journal, you will have entered into a study of the more hidden aspects of the self, and messages from the DPs will almost certainly happen from time to time. The more practiced you become at observing and remembering your dreams, the more adept you will become at recognizing their meanings. A tool that was suggested to me as support in reconnecting to your dreams, especially if you have trouble doing so, is to take a full glass of water to bed with you at night. Just before slipping off to sleep, drink half the glass, and affirm to yourself, and those who might make contact with you while you're dreaming, that when you wake up in the morning and drink the remaining half of the water, you will be connected to remembering the dream and its circumstances/messages/symbolism.

If you do decide to give dreams and dream journaling a try, you must commit to it for the same duration of weeks as your other practices. Commitment will be for getting up a half hour earlier to write down everything you can remember. Eventually, your body will adjust and end your dreams in time for you to awaken when you want. You might, in a short while, need more than a half hour for recalling because soon you will begin to remember more and more—including greater amounts of detail. You must give dream journaling its time to work its *magic*. Please keep another point in mind: if your dream is one in which the loved one is still in pain, distraught, ill, or injured, it is not a contact speaking, it is your own fears cropping up.

Ingredient # 5: Developing Subconscious Awareness

For this exercise, you will be writing letters using your non-dominant hand. That is, if you are right-handed, you will be using your left hand, and if you are left-handed, you will be using your right. These are not letters that will ever be sent anywhere; they are simply part of the practice of revealing hidden parts of your psyche. The purpose here is not to improve your penmanship! In

Signs from nature, like dreams, can reveal many things.

fact, it will feel strange and awkward, and the words will look much like a child's scrawl. That's okay. You don't really have to be able to read every word. You can choose to write to any or all of the names on your inventory list. The more often you do these kinds of exercises, the more comfortable you'll become with receiving and recognizing intuitive information. There is no need to make a great effort to think of things to say. The idea is to let the things that need to be said reveal themselves in a flow of ideas—a stream of consciousness. Any of these letters you choose to write should be written on a pad of paper—NOT in any other journal. You might want to purchase a larger artist's drawing pad, so you'll have plenty of space—non-dominant handwriting tends to be larger than your normal script. Any insightful or meaningful passages could be copied down in your other journals later, if you would like. Keep the pen moving, and try not to filter or edit anything that pops up. If you feel unpleasant emotions rising up inside, give them a voice, express them in words as best you can. You can always go back and extract the most significant parts to record later.

As you can see from the following list of possible kinds of letters, some are addressed to DPs, and some are addressed to yourself at a younger age, however old you were at the time of passing of your DP. There is no need to limit yourself to this list. Writing letters to aspects of your self at various ages in the non-dominant hand is a powerful tool in discovering the source of subconscious voices that often guide our choices without our being aware of it.

The list:

If the DP has passed within the past seven years, write a letter telling him or her everything you never had a chance to say. Ask any questions you have about his or her life and passing. Tell the DP what impact the event of the passing had on your life. Ask any questions you have about what he or she is doing in the afterlife.

> **Be on the lookout for a pet similar or familiar to a loved one that may cross your path.**

If the DP passed before you were fully grown, write a letter—from your present point of view—to yourself at the age you were when he or she passed. Comfort the DP, and tell them how everything turned out.

Now imagine the younger you replying to your letter. Let him or her tell you what it was like at the time; let that younger person spill his or her heart out to you. This is a powerful process you may want to try a few times to uncover what was buried, especially if your grieving process was interrupted or prevented in any way.

If the DP was not fully grown when he or she passed, write a letter to that person at the age they were at the time.

Then write a letter to the person you imagine he or she would have become today had he or she continued to grow.

If at any time you have a sense that the DP is trying to reply to you, write down whatever it is you think he or she might want to say. Even if you think you are making up what they would be saying, write it down anyway. Often this will be, or will become, an actual contact. Using the non-dominant hand allows this dictation to occur with the least chance that your conscious mind will be able to block or interfere with the process. While writing these letters, cultivate a level of detachment that allows you to observe yourself writing. The mental trick of stepping outside yourself to observe the process of your writing will allow the subconscious to reach the page. Do not filter or edit your words, and always use the non-dominant hand, unless you are copying something profound into another one of your journals.

Pictures of yourself, the family member, or whoever is the subject of your writing, taken around the time of the loss, are a great tool to use—one that readily triggers memories and connection. Place those pictures before you and spend some time just looking at them before you begin to write. This is a strong aid to creating "memory associations."

Ingredient #6: Adding the Spice of Nature

Nature is always talking to us, continually showing us signs of one kind or another. Put another way, our *unseen helpers,* including DPs, are good at getting nature's help. But, most of us go through our days in a haze, and miss most of what goes on in them. The ones that do get our attention are usually dramatic, so we tend to think they are uncommon. Hardly! Signs from nature, like dreams, can reveal many things. In the same way that a dream journal only assists in recalling dreams, the signs from nature must first be apprehended, and then interpreted. Then with any luck at all, the signs will be important and useful. Often, I have felt the guiding hand of the DPs as they somehow managed to arrange random events so that they are beneficial to soul growth among the living. Well, when the DPs, or any of our guides from the "unseen realms," want to get our attention, they also enlist their buddies among the birds and the bees, the flora and fauna, to help them do so. Alliances with animals and plants on a spiritual level have been happening for centuries, and are still possible in modern times. There is a lot to be learned from watching closely for signs in the natural world, especially when events occur that are just enough out of the ordinary. A sign could even come in the form of a sudden gust of wind at a poignant part of a conversation. Nature is a Master Chef when it comes to knowing how to nurture and support us. If you have done any studies around Native American cultures, you will have a head start understanding how Mother Earth sustains us.

If you are seeking contact with a deceased love one, remind yourself of the answers to the following exercise. If there are some answers you don't have, find out from someone who does. You can write these down under the list you made in the Inventory Process.

Exercise for Using Nature as a Guide:

- What was the DP's favorite animal? Or, in your family, were there aversions to animals? What were the causes for them, i.e. fears, allergies, etc.?

- If the deceased was a male, was he a hunter? What was his favorite thing to hunt—deer, elk, turkey, pheasant, or geese? Where did he most like to go hunting? Was he a fisherman? What was his favorite fish to catch? Where did he like to go fishing the most?

- Was the DP a gardener or farmer? What did he or she most like to grow? Did he or she have a favorite flower or plant?

- Do you associate the DP with a special place in memory? Write about this place.

- What were the DP's favorite types of places to get in touch with nature? Was he or she a mountain climber, beachcomber, or camper/explorer? Did he or she enjoy being outdoors at all?

The appearance in your life of any of these types of reminders may not be coincidental. In other words, they might be significant signals from your loved one, especially when repeated over a short period of time, or when they occur in a series of three. These signs need not occur only "outdoors" because nature is everywhere. Photos from magazines, as I have said, or even commercials on television can have personal significance. One of the signals commonly used to reach mortals with reminders from the beyond is fragrance. A sudden whiff of cologne or perfume, specifically floral scents such as lilac or rose, could be a DP reaching out. Even a waft of tobacco smoke from a pipe or cigar can bring a flood of memory and a connection.

The smells of traditional foods *out of nowhere* can actually be from *somewhere*—and I don't mean the neighbor's apartment. If nobody could make a sauce like grandma, she just might be cooking up a reminder to get you to notice that she is around. Smells are powerful, emotional triggers, and are used by DPs to get our attention because they bypass the conscious mind, similar to appearances in dreams. There are also negative smells that can call us into connection, such as those in hospitals or those that remind us of disease.

Be on the lookout for a pet similar or familiar to a loved one that may cross your path. Say you're sitting on a park bench, and someone comes by walking a dog just like a beloved pet once owned by your DP. The dog stops to sniff you, and the owner remarks how odd this behavior is and says something like, "she never goes up to strangers like that." Oh yes, you have most likely had a visit. Even if this specific scenario does not happen to you, it is an example of the kinds of possible situations that can occur if we are watchful and alert. Aside from the simple appearance of birds or animals—especially butterflies and hummingbirds— pay close attention to what they are doing. Is anything about the behavior unusual? Or if you don't know what normal behavior for them might be, do you sense anything odd about the appearance or the behavior? Sometimes proximity is part of a sign; a bird that flies too close to your head, lands unusually close, or squawks loudly while you are talking, might just be on a spiritual errand for someone.

Exercise—Nature Notes:

Use a journal to write down at the end of a day every animal or bird that caught your attention. So much happens in nature that we never consciously see, that you may be quite surprised at how much you do see once you start noticing. Keep in mind that the discipline of expanding our powers of observation is the same discipline that can improve our connections with the unseen realms.

By writing "nature notes" every evening in a journal, and your dreams in the morning, you might begin to see that the hidden aspects of your subconscious gradually start bubbling up into your awareness—the same way dreams begin to reveal more and more of their truth to you.

Biologists keep a field journal of their observations, not only to remember what they saw, but also to improve their ability to see more in the first place. Consider your journaling of nature as your *cosmic field journal.* Some of your sightings will

. . . we must allow the need for perfection to go out the window.

not mean anything more than natural activity. The idea is to stretch your skills, start noticing the world around you, and become more aware of nature as an agency that holds many possibilities for contact from beyond.

What are the birds and animals doing when they cross your path? Are they looking at you directly? Paying more attention to you than they normally would? Just write everything down without trying to deduce meaning immediately. This practice will increase your observational skills, but, even more, you may find that your senses and your intuition are developing as well.

A closing thought to those of you who live in cities. I know that cities have parks, whether large or small, so I know you can find a place to have experiences with nature. I live in New York City, and I love to stroll through Central Park. I have found places in that park that most people don't even know exist. It is a wonderful place to explore and connect. And there are playgrounds! Watch the children play and see what comes to mind. Some of you are in cities that are near oceans, lakes, or rivers. Go there! Water is a great conductor for connection. There are those of you who are near mountains and deserts. These, too, are great places to enhance your senses, and expand your awareness. So, get out there and look, smell, touch, taste, and come alive!

> *Let us never underestimate the impact that sounds can have on us.*

Resources:
Animal-Speak: The Spiritual & Magical Powers of Creatures Great & Small by **Ted Andrews**:
Llewellyn Publications; 1st ed edition (October 1, 1993)

Medicine Cards : The Discovery of Power Through the Ways of Animals by **Jamie Sams, David Carson, Angela C. Werneke**:
St. Martin's Press; Rev Bk&Crd edition (July 30, 1999)

Animal Wisdom by **Jessica Dawn Palmer**:
Thorsons Publishers (July 1, 2001)

Ingredient #7: Art for Inspiration

Art and the act of creating art are wonderful *soul connectors*. Any combination of art and making art can be a key that opens a door of connection to a loved one—a door that has been locked for some time. Please do not create a block for yourself by saying, "But, I'm not an artist." We are *all* artists. We are creating constantly, and creativity is part of who we are. We are creating our thoughts, lives, relationships, *and* connections from the time we get out of bed in the morning right up to the time we drift into sleep at night—and there, too. Creativity is our natural state of being. Our lives are our art. So, whether you choose one ingredient or another to complete your recipe, you are ultimately being the "artist," creating your own banquet. It can be as elaborate and spectacular, or as simple and unassuming as you like. Just be truthful to yourself and it will be deliciously unique. In our attempts to make connections, we will want to be as creative as we can. It might have been that when you were growing up, you were not encouraged to be creative. A lot of us are adult children of parents who experienced America's Great Depression, and whose lives were about being practical, sensible, and not taking risks. Security was the key issue, and often routines were set with no room for change.

At the same time, art and making art may have been all around you, but you did not realize it could be called that. Think about it. Did any of your family knit, sew, crochet, weave, play games, make up stories, create sculptures, make collections, write poetry, grow lovely gardens, carve wood, or make a special lure for fishing? I could go on and on. We are so often conditioned to not see these kinds of activities as creating art. Giving yourself "permission" to have an artistic experience is the beginning of *thinking outside the box*—critical to the work we are doing here.

You might say to yourself at this point, "Okay, I'll give it a try, but where do I start?" Let me give you some ideas to look into.

- Go to a museum, any museum. Notice what captures your attention. If it is a painting, what about it interests you? If it is a landscape, what in particular caused you to stop and take a longer look? If it is the artist who created the painting that intrigues you, what about him or her intrigues you? This might stir up your sense of connection to a loved one.

- Color! You can start exploring color anywhere you are comfortable. Some of the best triggers have been experienced through a box of crayons and a children's coloring book. And, you don't have to stay within the lines this time! Or, purchase a sketchpad and just draw whatever comes to mind. A great help in freeing yourself up is playing some favorite music as an accompaniment while you color and sketch.

- Create a scrapbook of your favorite things. Cut pictures, any pictures that touch you in some way, and place them on the scrapbook pages to create collages that speak to you—pages that form a special statement about you *or* a loved one.

- If you have a box of old snapshots tucked away that you have wanted to do something with, you can also arrange these in a photo album in a way that tells a story. Photos are great ways to make connections.

Rearrange a room to your liking. Create a special place in it for yourself. Maybe you want to establish an area—a sacred place—that is yours for practicing some of the ingredients you learn here. One where you are in a safe atmosphere and free from ridicule. (As I said earlier, it is important for you to decide very carefully with whom and also what you will share about the work you are doing.)

Go to an outdoor art show or street fair, and pay attention to what and where you are drawn.

The primary idea here is to give you permission to *participate in the art of creating* in some way. If you do this, you will become more open to the possibilities of connection and you may have some kind of breakthrough. I once heard someone say, "We are taught to hide the colors of our *full* self." I believe this to be true. To begin to open up that creative artist who is stretching toward cooking up a great banquet of connections, we must allow the need for perfection to go out the window. The need for perfection usually leads to

When movement is in play, shifts occur.

procrastination, which can, in turn, lead to paralysis. In the end, we do nothing at all because we feel we cannot do it perfectly. Stop now, and give yourself permission to explore.

Ingredient #8: Underscoring Your Life with Music

There is nothing more beautiful than the transforming power of music; it is far more than just a source of entertainment. I think of it as an essential food that nourishes us everyday. Beautiful music that resonates with us can be a distinctive tool for healing and extended spiritual consciousness. There is nothing that goes directly to a "soul connection" more than great music. Music is all about connection, connection, and connection.

Many fine musicians today are coming to understand just how powerful the healing energies of music are. We see concerts like the recent *Live 8, 2005* where many musicians gathered to promote a certain healing atmosphere on this planet. There are artists, Tim Wheater for one, who are using musical tones and writing lyrics to produce works for healing. A good example is Wheater's CD called *Heart Land.* One cannot be too emphatic that music communes with our soul. Each of us has certain music or songs that instantly trigger memories. Usually when we hear a tune or a lyric, we are momentarily transported to another place and time.

. . . once you begin to open up, the messages can come from anywhere.

Sometimes music envelopes us with soothing, nurturing feelings of love and joy, and sometimes engulfs us with sadness, melancholy, and loss. Some music may lift or calm our spirits; other kinds may agitate us.

Hal A. Lingerman, in his book, *The Healing Energies of Music* (which I encourage you to read), says, "I believe music can be one such catalyst for good. Music is an extremely important instrument of the Divine. When it is used wisely and effectively, music will attune [us] to higher sources of love and power, thus strengthening [our] character and goals, and giving [us] increased spiritual purpose on earth."

Also, Richard Wagner, known for his operas of ancient German myths, has said that music is the universal language. I believe this to be true. It is a universal language that traverses all the boundaries that may separate us. Because everyone responds to music, it is a connector. So, one of your greatest ingredients/ tools to use for practicing connecting is music.

Take some time to listen to some of your favorite music. For an even greater experience, listen to some music that you are not familiar with and see what emotions/feelings are brought up. Create a time and place where you can "breathe in" its message uninterrupted. Let it take you wherever it may, and notice where it is taking you. After it is over, give yourself some time to sit in silence to internalize how the music "spoke to you." Did it make you feel energized, calm, anxious, courageous, or adventuresome? Did it give you a sense of hope or send you into despair? Pay attention to the emotions that it aroused. Also, did some special time, place, or loved one come to mind? What did that bring up for you? Ask yourself if you could possibly have had a connection?

Different instruments speak to specific parts of our "framework." As I have learned from Lingerman, brass, percussion, heavy sounds of bass notes, electronic music (most of it) speak to our physical bodies, woodwinds and strings to our emotional selves. Strings also speak to our mental parts, harp and organ, wind chimes, and high strings, speak strongly to our souls. So, play music; dance to music; sing; or hum with music; make art to music; write to music; or, just "be" with music. However you choose to experience music, and whatever music you select, let it flow through you and become a connector. As Lingerman suggests, "If you take time to prepare yourself beforehand for your music, it will play through you, not just around you."

Let me take a moment to speak about the power of sounds in general. Without them, we would have no music; there would be no underscoring of our emotions when watching TV shows, movies, and commercials, plays, and sports events. For example, the sounds of the spectacular opening and closing of the Olympic games rev us all up. The impact and impressions we get from all of

Even if you think nothing has happened while practicing any or all of these ingredients, don't give up.

these experiences are enhanced by sound. Do you ever think about the sound of a loved one's voice once he or she is gone? What was it like—soothing, harsh, annoying, or shrill? Was it a voice whose sound drew you closer, or one that you trusted or feared, or when hearing it, did you have the impulse to run? Let us never underestimate the impact that sounds can have on us. So, I urge you to open yourself to the healing capacities of sounds as well as music.

Ingredient #9: Movement

There is no more pleasurable feeling than having the sense that you are grounded in your body. If you are not consistently involved in some kind of movement, your body will tighten up and that feeling of tightness will permeate your life. Like any ingredient/tool we intend to engage in regularly in our practice, if we don't exercise our muscles, our bodies will tend to atrophy. So it is with the tools we are calling our "ingredients" here. Even if you have been blessed with a wonderful body, you must keep it "well-oiled" for the parts to work at their best and in harmony. Movement can come in all sizes, shapes, and packages: walking, running, swimming, dancing, stretching, other workout activities, having massages, taking part in sports, most outdoor activities, and many more that I haven't mentioned.

I believe also that laughter brings a great deal of movement to our bodies; it engages the body fully. Movement can be as wildly physical as that of a *whirling dervish* or as gentle as some *yoga* practices. Both are powerful. But for exploring deep levels, there is no tool more powerful than movement combined with conscious breathing. It is important to keep in mind what the definition of movement is. In fact, the American Heritage Dictionary (Fourth Edition) gives movement several definitions. Here are five of them:

1. The act or an instance of moving; a change in place or position.

2. A series of actions and events taking place over a period of time and working to foster a principle or policy: a movement toward world peace.

3. A tendency or trend: a movement toward larger kitchens. [Hello!]

4. The suggestion or illusion of motion in a painting, sculpture, or design.

5. The rhythmical or metrical structure of a poetic composition.

In considering these definitions, let's contemplate for a bit how they might be related to our learning how to connect. One meaning of movement is associated with the act of moving, making a change in place and/or position. As we engage in our practice of connecting, aren't we also shifting our consciousness to a new *place* of thinking and understanding? Aren't we working toward *positioning* ourselves to be more open to the possibilities of a deeper meaning to our lives and those we love? Aren't we also working toward living within a higher principle of peaceful existence? All of what we are doing here is an effort to create a larger *kitchen* so we can better understand and connect with our soul's program. As we work on becoming Master Chefs in our kitchens, aren't we painting, sculpturing, and designing a practice that will support our highest good: healing, and evolution spiritually? The *rhythm* in which we develop the consistency and *structure*—our menus that we wish to create—all have a sense of poetry in motion, don't they? You can see from these questions and their answers as well, that we are already involved in a movement that will ultimately have great effect on our lives. When movement is in play, shifts occur. Aren't you excited!

Try doing some of these movement activities:

- Take a walk and pay attention to your breath going in and out as you do. Breathe in the smells around you.
- Put some music on and dance. Or even better, take a dance class: tap, jazz, ballet, or ballroom.
- Take an exercise class: Tai Chi, swimming, or yoga.
- Do some stretches to music at home.

Find and attend a group that does "free dancing."

Go out and ride a bike.

Get a massage. (Yes, massage is movement. It moves the body around.)

Ingredient #10: Association as a Practice to Open Up

As we attempt to attune our awareness to all our senses, we have discussed practices we can do that plunges us into creative activities: art, writing, and nature, into a world of sounds and music much larger than we are used to, practices that help us to notice smells, the feel of things (touch) and what we see. The heightened awareness of the senses can bring an increase in the possibilities for associations they may have for us (usually long forgotten) that may lead to a connection.

I want to take a moment to elaborate on another aspect of association that can be heightened when you begin to practice these tools, and that is one related to elements—the textures present in our lives. When I speak of "elements," I am talking about the tangibles around you like metal, wood, glass, clay, and fabric that you come in contact with everyday. For our purposes in this context, I will translate those into products we interact with like bowls, utensils, cookware, dishes, table settings, tablecloths, and napkins. And, we can extend this to furniture, clothing, etc.

As our senses are expanded, we might find that there is an attraction to certain elements because of a connection to some loved one or memory of the past. For example, over the years of doing my work, I find that I prefer wooden bowls and chopsticks, as a rule, for salads. There is something about the texture of these that enhances my enjoyment of the dish, and gives connection to my past. So, you might want to take a look at the elements you are drawn to as a possible connection to a loved one. For instance, have you ever been out shopping and suddenly become drawn to a particular item that brings forth a thought of a loved one who has passed—a memory of a time together? This could be a message. Or maybe you go to a new restaurant and find an unexpected item on the menu that has special meaning to your family dining and a loved one. What I'm trying to say is that once you begin to open up, the messages can come from anywhere. Stay aware, always.

Our goal in practicing some, a combination, or all of the ingredients/tools offered here, and especially when combined with conscious breathing, is to give each of us a better chance of igniting a connection.

Be prepared to use the associations that arise to aid you in making a connection to a loved one who has passed on.

A note on adding your own ingredients:

While I am encouraging you to explore ingredients that expand your conscious efforts for connecting, there is one I want to caution you about: *stay away from the Ouija Board!* The Ouija Board, in and of itself, has no power. In using it, however, you give clear access into your mind and thoughts to *any* person in the spirit world who wants to come through, including unhappy souls from the Astral Realm, or ghosts. In other words, just don't use the Ouija Board. We do not want to "mix" it in with our recipes. Its elements are not harmonious with what we are trying to create.

Keep on keeping on

Even if you think nothing has happened while practicing any or all of these ingredients, *don't give up*. Remember that you're committed, and by practicing your relaxation and visualization techniques, you'll gradually become more comfortable with and open to the process and the meaning of what you have been experiencing. You are already receiving messages whether you can believe it now or not. Don't be surprised if within the next few days, you begin to "hear," with your greater sense of listening, a message when you least expect it. If it happens so fleetingly that you're not even sure it occurred at all, let it go. The DPs don't give up easily, and the next message you may receive will be easier for you to grasp. You might also experience some other kind of symbolic connection that lets you know your loved one has received your invitation. As I've said, electronic or mechanical disturbances are among the most common signals the DPs send to remind us of their presence. Or you might notice unusual natural phenomena—flowers blooming out of season or birds appearing when and where they never have before. You might, in fact, have experienced those things at other times and never paid much attention simply because you weren't "tuned in" to their significance. I would like you to think about an insight of Claudia Black's, the author of *Changing Course: Healing from Loss, Abandonment, and Fear,* as you continue to explore connecting and communicating on your own. I rather like it.

"Trust in yourself. Your perceptions are often far more accurate than you are willing to believe."

RECIPE CARD:

What "ingredients" did you work with easily?

Practice the ingredients/tools consistently.

Journal about what you are experiencing.

CHAPTER SEVEN:

Embracing Your "Inner Cook" and Creating Your Own Banquet for Connection

Have faith, and let the self-worth grow

Have you noticed that all these ingredients and tools are relatively simple to do? When practicing them, you are asked to open yourself to the adventure and keep a sense of humor. You are asked, also, to maintain a willingness to open the doors that lead to your carefully protected inner self, and to listen *inwardly as well as* outwardly. By heightening your conscious awareness, you'll gain as a person and as a receiver of the DPs' love. As you increase your ability to do the exercises, you will increase your faith in yourself, in what you are capable of being, and in your capability to make communication happen. The DPs are waiting for you to astound yourself and say, "Hey, I can do this! It works! I need to stay on the course."

For the most successful results at any level, you will need to become secure in the knowledge that, beyond a doubt, God or a Higher Power is guiding and protecting you. You'll also need to maintain a realistic perspective on what can and cannot happen. Stay rooted in your expanding conscious awareness.

How to begin creating your banquet

You have learned and begun to practice some new techniques. Some of these will feel comfortable immediately, some will take time to get comfortable with, and some will not seem to work for you. So, what do you do from this point on? Take what does work, let go of the rest for now, and begin to use these new tools on a regular basis. What does work can be the new "comfort foods" for you, and you can add them to your menu—what you bring to your banquet table. Now a new sense of self-confidence about making connections begins to unfold. As with anything, some days may be great and others may present a challenge. Change your combination of ingredients around from time to time to see what might work the best for you, especially if you are feeling some resistance. The important piece to all of this practice is consistency, and if you come to the "kitchen" daily with your new recipes, working with an array of ingredients, you will recognize a wonderful shift taking place in your confidence and ability to make connections.

> **The important piece to all of this practice is consistency...**

This is all about you giving yourself permission to create exactly what works for you. This is your menu, and your banquet. If something is not working, make a change; most importantly, take the time to examine *why* it is not working for you. Is there some issue still lingering in relation to the loved one you are trying to contact? Of course you know you have to examine that first. Some days you will want something quick and easy for your meal, and other days you may become excited about creating a sumptuous recipe. Just remember, using the ingredients that work best for you in any preparation brings the best results. It is your choice what you decide to use. Also, I hope you have come to realize that "skimping" on the recipe does not work.

As the Master Chef and adventurer, it is up to you how grand a way or how simple a recipe you will choose to explore on a given day. By this time, you should have an air of confidence bubbling up from within. If you have been steadily approaching your "cooking" with preparation—mental and physical—then you are probably beginning to have a feeling of comfort about what you are trying to accomplish. By this time, you have tested the recipes, made some changes so that they work for your tastes, and you are most likely experiencing some connections. Once you have begun to work with your tools consistently in this process, you will come to realize that you are continually "tuning up" and activating your spiritual/psychic centers. These centers are called *chakras,* a Sanskrit word that means "wheels." When you are in a committed practice, you are activating spiritual energy which travels the route of the chakras, from the base of the spine up through to the base of the brain where all paranormal/psychic activity occurs. One of the reasons for consistent practice is that it activates this energy that can lead to greater psychic awareness. So, choose what you want to bring into your kitchen carefully to begin to prepare your banquet.

Creating an atmosphere for success

Just as it is important to choose the best ingredients for the recipes you prepare, it is also important to give attention to the setting in which you plan to "cook." As you learned in the chapter called *The Main Ingredients*, how you prepare the space you work in can

> *Create your own ceremony to celebrate what you are about to do . . .*

have a strong impact on the quality of your creation. I trust that by now you have created for yourself a sacred space where you are comfortable exploring—critically important when you are ready to "cater" a banquet. This will be another step in strengthening your courage. When you arrive at this point, it is important to "anchor" yourself in some way before you begin. Create your own ceremony to celebrate what you are about to do: play a special musical piece in the background, light candles, or say a prayer. Do whatever works for you to center yourself and create a safe atmosphere. You decide what you will to bring to the table, and whatever you choose will be just right. Also think about how you want to serve it. After all, a banquet is a ceremonial dinner prepared for a special occasion. It is something well prepared and enjoyed—and *you* are the chef in charge of the whole affair.

> **No one can give you faith, self-confidence, or self-worth.**

As you continue to wake up your "inner cook," you will learn with practice what works for you. Some days you might want one ingredient, and some days another. You get to decide what to mix together or keep separate. Some days you may want to prepare an assortment of "dishes," and other days you may feel that cutting back serves you better. There will be days when you feel a stronger need to use one ingredient over another. Go with it. And there will be other days when you are just not sure what you want, so you might need to do a "taste test" to discover what is best for you that day. It is all about giving yourself permission to cook, eat, and set the table according to your desires. This is where your individuality begins to emerge. Ultimately, your banquet will be all your own. Even if it is similar to others, it will *not* be the same as anyone else.

On some days you will be confident about your decisions, and on others you will reach for the "comfort food." No matter what you choose to create, the combinations are up to you. Make changes when you feel they are necessary—don't compromise— just allow yourself to add or omit certain ingredients until the "taste" is just the way you want it. It is all about creating your own shopping list when you go to the "store," and remember that combining recipes is perfectly okay. Set the table as you wish, adorning it with anything that pleases you. Experiment. Don't be afraid to take charge in your own kitchen!

No one can give you faith, self-confidence, or self-worth. If you lack it, a large chunk of life will be more difficult. Certainly contact with the DPs will be more difficult. I am quite sure we all have some kernel of faith somewhere inside ourselves that stays there unappreciated. Do not be *afraid* that it is not there. With rare exception, it is our fears—actually, an accumulation of fears—that get in the way. Keep this old story in mind, "Fear knocked on the door, Faith and Self-Worth opened it and no one was there"—at least that is the way I like to remember it. So, write your own menu and create your own banquet. Someone may already be waiting to taste your meal!

Exercise:

1. Once a day, take the time to get quiet and practice one tool you have learned.
2. Identify what tools are working best for you.
3. Create a scenario of a banquet in which you celebrate and engage in a combination of tools.
4. Journal how this experience was for you and what happened.

RECIPE CARD:

 Bring conscious awareness to your "inner cook" by journaling your experiences.

 Create atmospheres for success.

 Explore the combinations you can use in preparing your own banquet.

Don't Give Up if You Burn It!
What to Do When You Hit the Wall

When the messages stop

You may find you are a natural connector and are having great results in all your efforts until one day things stop. Maybe you were on a "roll" and then you hit a wall or fell into a slump. This, too, is part of the journey. Getting out of your own way is important. If you find yourself becoming discouraged, stop trying so hard! Internalize the notion that developing these gifts is everyone's birthright. Perhaps it is better not to think about this as developing anything at all, but rather as a process of removing the constrictions that keep your natural abilities from revealing themselves and flourishing.

Once you've been successful in connecting with the DPs, either on your own or with the help of a medium, you will certainly want the messages to continue. You will probably assume that if your loved one came to you once, he or she will undoubtedly do so again. It is certainly possible that this will happen, particularly if you really *need* to continue the contact in order to complete your grieving or come to terms with some aspect of your relationship that was unfinished on the earthly plane—often true when a parent has lost a child. The loss of a child is, without a doubt, one of the most devastating losses anyone can sustain. You will want so desperately to make a connection to them. However, connections in general happen on special occasions, such as holidays, birthdays, and anniversaries, which would be your loved one's way of letting you know that he or she knows that it is a special day and that they are still aware of what is happening in your life.

Once you have made a connection with the DPs, it can be very seductive because it can be mixed so easily with grieving and longing for the departed, especially, if their passing was recent. We can cling to the desire to hold on to the departed one and resist letting go of the connection because it has become a source of reassurance.

It is also possible that after one or two contacts, your DP will not be there for you again. I don't know exactly why this happens, but I do know that it happens for a reason that we may not understand at the moment. Perhaps your DP just needed to assure you that he or she loved you and was still a presence in your life; having delivered that message, there was no more for them to say. Perhaps the DP needed to move on with his or her own soul's growth and evolution, just as you need to let go and move on with your own. You may find it hard to come to grips with or understand that the DPs have work they must complete. You will no doubt be disappointed if your contacts are cut off, but you should not be discouraged. Remember that before you began these contacts, you gave yourself over to the Higher Power and vowed that you were acting in the highest good. It is simply not up to you to decide just when that good will be accomplished. The point of connecting is *not* to keep on receiving reassurances, but to help us let go of the deceased and get on with our own lives.

If you find yourself becoming discouraged, stop trying so hard!

There are, also, times when it is beneficial to step away, and give yourself a break from it all. This may be a signal that you need to become centered and grounded in your inner truth once again. On these occasions, take the time to review the notes and records in your journals. Strive to integrate the lessons all the more, instead of avoiding them because of some shift in the regularity of

> ***One of the most important, but often overlooked, steps in learning to connect is called*** **integration.**

contact. One of the most important, but often overlooked, steps in learning to connect is called *integration*. This particular step needs to occur every time we have moved ahead on a steep learning curve. After any lesson or experience we consider deep or expansive, we need to stop and rest to let it all sink in. It just may be that doing this intense work has led you to feeling like you are "cooking" too much or living in a "pressure cooker."

On the other hand, hitting a "wall" could mean that you have become so obsessive in your practice that you are blocking the very issues or situations you are seeking to resolve or heal, that you are actually creating more stress in your life. This could be a hint that there is something that you are not yet ready to release. When we give ourselves over to this deep work, sometimes we can find ourselves getting caught up in such unproductive thoughts as, "Am I doing it right? Or wrong? Or, I'm not making enough progress." Like having climbed a difficult and challenging mountain, reaching the top and needing to rest, admiring the view, and absorbing the exhilarating accomplishment, you want to integrate your new, expanded awareness from your lessons into your way of being in the world. This is not the time to forge ahead with new learning, it is time to rest and savor your fresh perspective and the wisdom you have gained strengthening your Soul Program and letting it permeate your life. Allowing time for this integration step helps you retain the learning, and prepare yourself to absorb the steps ahead.

Because many of us are driven achievers, we don't always recognize the best times to take a break ...

Because many of us are driven achievers, we don't always recognize the best times to take a break; we can also be thrown off balance by the intensity of our grief. The DPs are making time for this necessary rest by giving us a pause in the action. This kind of a breather can prevent our path of discovery from becoming a relentless quest, and can help minimize obsessive or self-destructive tendencies. But, despite the pauses, don't give up!

Overcooking and undercooking

There are other reasons we can sometimes hit a wall while undertaking this practice. So, as the chef, you may be asking yourself, "Did I overcook or undercook the recipe?" "Did I leave it in too long, or take out it too soon?" "Did I set the temperature too high or too low?" or "Why doesn't this taste right?" All of these are reasonable questions to ponder when you are starting out on this journey of connecting.

Here are some ideas that you might explore about why you are having this challenging moment:

- Maybe you are having trouble getting beyond the illness of the loved one who has passed over.

- Perhaps you are holding on to the memories of when the relationship with the DP was not good.

Often there is a conflict or rivalry that still exists among you and your siblings having to do with a passed parent who may have loved one of you more than the others, or who preferred the child or children of one sex over the other: i.e., either the boys or girls were more important.

Or, I was the outcast. I was banished. My parent did not like me anyway.

I could never do enough or do "it" well enough.

I am not worthy of having a connection with them.

> ***Forgiveness sends us directly to compassion and from there we connect with love.***

If any of this is bringing you to a halt, do stop and take a rest. Try to remember a time when things *were* good in the relationship with your DP, and allow yourself to remain with that memory for a while. This is a good time to work on forgiving yourself and the loved one so that you can move on. If being disconnected from your family for some reason is ruining your recipe for connection, give yourself permission to change those memory images that you no longer want to have running around in your head. Begin now by inventing the kind of family you think you would want. When you feel more at peace with the dynamics of your birth family—and that only comes by doing your work on a deep level—then return to your "kitchen." Remember forgiveness is the underlying theme of all that we are doing. Forgiveness sends us directly to compassion and from there we connect with love. Once there, we are on the road to healing.

A note about the "other" walls

Sometimes it may feel like we are blocked by another kind of wall made up of the negativities and alarms of others toward what we are doing. They may be engaging us with a "prove it to me" attitude. The fear and anxiety this causes are wall builders. If you resist by putting up a wall against them, you lose. Other reasons walls can be created are overindulgence, addictive behavior, and, as I have pointed out before, by placing yourself in a vulnerable position because you chose to work in a place that is not safe enough. Also, there will be times your emotions—despair, hatred, fear, rage, envy, frustration, abandonment, self-pity—are so strong and raw that the DP is unable to come through clearly. He or she will back away for now, realizing that what he or she needs to say cannot be said, or heard,

Take a day off and allow yourself some time to do something you truly enjoy.

at this time. As you become more adept in dealing with your issues, everything will once again come together, and you will find yourself in a renewed state of joy. You will delight in this recognition, and also weep as you realize the freedom you have gained by letting go and healing your pains.

There is a final reason why nothing is happening for you during an attempt at communication. It may be that this particular time, the communication is just not meant to be—for now—but not forever. If that is the case, it is in the hands of your Higher Source—a truth we may not want to hear. Usually, however, it is the exception; most of us, almost always, will make some form of contact. So, don't throw away the recipes you have created. Just take a break and practice some "First Aid cooking."

First Aid cooking

Before anything else, be patient with yourself. This process of connection, "cooking up" communications with those who have *passed over*, may bring up many disturbing emotions, resistances, and conflicts. Be honest with yourself and how you are doing with these factors in relation to your process. It might be time to revisit your inventory. Deal with your fears and beliefs, but, also be gentle

> *Give yourself plenty of healthy nurturing as you go along.*

and nurturing with yourself. You don't have to solve every problem immediately, just acknowledge what you are feeling at the moment, especially by writing it down. Remember, challenging your fears and beliefs is healthy; constantly analyzing and rationalizing them is not. It is also quite acceptable and desirable to ask for help. Give yourself a break and possibly lighten the atmosphere a little by trying some of your other ingredients/tools. Have some fun!

For starters, take a look at your eating habits. Are they healthy? Are your sleep routines and exercise on track, or out of sync? These are some key ingredients to maintaining your practice at its best. Take a day off and allow yourself some time to do something you truly enjoy. Is there something you love to do that you have been putting off? Do it! There are many ways to nurture and reconnect with yourself, some of which have been examined in the chapter on "The Main Ingredients." Here are a few "First Aid" tips to help you reconnect and return to your center:

- How long has it been since you have done any artwork?

- If you enjoy walking or hiking at the beach, in the mountains, wilderness, or desert, when was the last time you took some time to do it? Do it now! When you are there smell the aromas, listen to the sounds, and see the surroundings with new wonder.

- Do you have a book that you have been putting off reading just for fun? If so, get it and place yourself in a special place and start it.

- Music, music, music! Dance, sing, or just sit and listen. Remember what music can do for the soul.

- Visit a museum. There must be one that has something of interest to you.

- Write poetry. Allow whatever comes out of your soul to express itself on paper.

- Literally cook! Prepare your favorite meal, or go to your favorite restaurant. And yes, you can enjoy the experience on your own!

- Go to a botanical garden or purchase some flowers and design an arrangement just for yourself. Of course, when doing this "First Aid" tip, remember to breathe deeply. Immerse yourself in the aromatic scents around you.

- Go to a place that is sacred to you—experience it in silence. A sacred place can be wherever you choose. Be an explorer!

- Do something with your hands. Do you like to garden? How about a class in working with clay?

Exercising in a gym can be nurturing for some people. Have you been sedentary of late? Get the body moving.

Practice the "art of wandering," as Joseph Campbell calls it. Go some place you have not been to and just allow yourself to wander with no purpose at all. Just be in the environment.

If you like to drive, get in your car, choose a direction, and just go! Staying on back roads can keep the adventure at a low stress level, and the discoveries can be surprising and wonderful.

Sit outdoors and watch the clouds, or go to a playground and watch the children play.

You have now been given some explanations about why we sometimes hit walls—those times when nothing seems to happen. Choose what you want to use to help soften any frustration and angst that may come from hitting those walls. I hope you also understand that this happens to all of us. Do not end up abandoning the work. Above all, it is critical to honor your body, mind, and spirit. Give yourself plenty of healthy nurturing as you go along. Eat well, get plenty of rest, and take time for solitude. Keep reminding yourself that your Soul Program directed you here.

RECIPE CARD:

 Take breaks periodically to rest.

 Do something that gives you pleasure.

Journal your thoughts, and acknowledge the progress you have made.

Beyond the Pilot Light
—How to Keep Going

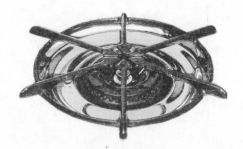

CHAPTER NINE

Taking Stock: What have You Done? What have You Accomplished?

B y now you should have some indication that you are making connections to your loved ones who have passed. The process that has allowed that to happen has been unique—yours only. Remember, if you think you have made a connection, you have! Don't question it, and don't let the fears or doubts of others get in the way of what you know has happened or *is* happening. You are stronger now. Here is a little story on how we can be affected by the outside influences in our lives if we don't make the effort to become aware of *who* we are, and *what* we are doing:

As a person who travels a great deal, I often spend a lot of time in restaurants, and I am always "experiencing" people and watching their actions. One morning while working on this book, I was in a hotel restaurant having breakfast and thinking about food and eating in relation to what I wanted to write. Across from me sat a mother and her son—an extremely handsome young man with long hair—waiting to have their orders taken. As the waitress approached from behind the young man, she greeted them with, "Good Morning Ladies." I immediately saw the young man stiffen and give the waitress and his mother a distressed look. The waitress, seeing her mistake, began to apologize far too profusely. The mother jumped in and said it was not a problem, and not to give it a thought. "That always happens," she said, trying to smooth the waters. Yet, the young man was still upset. When the waitress left, there were a few minutes of conversation between mother and son in which she tried to invalidate how he was feeling and what he heard. I could see that he thought his feelings were not being acknowledged, and an uncomfortable silence fell over the table until they finished and began to leave. As they passed my table, I said simply, "You are a very handsome man." He gave me a smile, said, "thank you," and left.

Believe it or not, the next morning I came into the same restaurant and across from me again sat an almost identical pair, echoing the previous morning's duo. And, if you think that the waitress had learned her lesson, you are mistaken. She committed the same faux pas as she had the day before. Now, the difference this time was that as she started her apology, they both just looked at her and smiled. The son said, "That's quite alright. I get that a lot because of my long hair." No one this morning seemed upset except the waitress. And, most interesting to me was that this mother did not jump in to speak for her son.

Whatever they were, his feelings were his own.

The reason I offer this story is to help you understand that some people around you are going to try to invalidate what you are experiencing while you are practicing to make connections. Restaurants are good places to observe the dynamics of families and relationships and the kind of energy circulating among them. Seeing such encounters has helped me to realize how we have come to feel that our experiences are invalid and that so many of us have been denied our own feelings and sensations. I urge you to believe that *if you feel you have had a contact, you very likely have.* Try to let go of the feeling that what you are experiencing cannot be what you think it is. Protect yourself not only from your internal invalidators, but also from those in your life who are still doing that to you.

If you are still not sure if you are making contact, do you at least feel you are getting closer? If not, then what might be in your way is a block that stubbornly won't go away. Perhaps it is time to seek support. I will talk about that in Chapters Ten and Twelve.

If you have made a connection, however, give yourself credit for your patience and perseverance. It is time to acknowledge all that you have accomplished. By now, you ought to have an expanded sense of self and awareness from your commitment to the consistent practice of the tools given in Chapter Six. After weeks of working to enhance your sense of awareness, it is time, for you to celebrate—yourself. I hope you have learned to no longer deprive yourself of the things your Soul Program calls for in your life. *As you continue to practice, you will become more attuned to what you need for your own healing.* I trust you now realize that the reason you came here was about much more than just making contact with a loved one who has passed over. I agree that your initial attraction to this book was probably about making that special connection to a loved one, but it is also about learning to use those parts of yourself that will provide a continuum for your own growth. Through the continued practice of the *ingredients* that you have learned and the *recipes* you have created, you will go on to find new resources to support your own spiritual journey. I hope you have discovered by now that one step taken toward the abundant Universe will

> **Try to let go of the feeling that what you are experiencing cannot be what you think it is.**

be returned to you ten-fold in support. When you hold on gently to your means of reasonable exploration, your spiritual expansion can begin. You can begin to comprehend how your thoughts (negative and positive) can influence your conscious awareness. What you focus on you will bring into your realm of being. Opening up to a deeper willingness to trust yourself will support your desires to make contact.

> *What you focus on you will bring into your realm of being.*

Living with this new feeling of awareness and having an expanded understanding of your senses, you will find that there is a deeper healing taking place than the one you initially came here to find. Also, you have probably come to enjoy the nurturing feeling that envelopes you from the periods of solitude you have set aside as your "alone time." For me, it is the most appetizing part of this preparation—somewhat like a great stock for a delicious soup. As you learn to become more comfortable in your own skin in all areas of your life, you will learn at the same time to handle yourself more graciously and independently, following your inner voice rather the suggestions and inclinations of others.

Those of you who will have the greatest success in making contact will be the ones who have approached the practice diligently even through moments of frustration, and questioning—not to mention just plain grief. What I know is that if you stay with this exploration, at some point you will turn a corner and begin to recognize you are making connections— to yourself and the DPs. As you become increasingly aware of your own needs and are taking positive steps to address them, you will receive another gift of this practice: the painful "hole" inside ourselves, that we have all felt at times, will begin to fill. This is a precious by-product of what you have been doing.

I know you will come to understand that all outside connections, here and beyond, are tempered by the relationship we have with ourselves. I see another cause to celebrate: you have given yourself permission to enter territories that were once forbidden—the world of

> ***Once you get beyond the anger and denial, forgiveness opens the door to compassion and understanding . . .***

spirit *and* your inner self. You are searching for a degree of hope where you would not think to look before, and most importantly, you are learning to come to forgiveness. As I am sure you realize by now, forgiveness is a major factor in healing ourselves and our relationships. If you are resistant to forgiving, your life will be a rough road, indeed. I know that sometimes it is hard to find a key to open the door to forgiveness, yet forgiveness—of yourself and others—is itself the key to resolution in your life. Once you get beyond the anger and denial, forgiveness opens the door to compassion and understanding, and that, as we now know, leads to healing. What you have accomplished in these last weeks has made you be a healthier co-creator of your life. We may live in a "Fast Food Society," but this work is clearly not for the burger and French fries crowd.

Taking time to acknowledge what you have learned about yourself

- What is your understanding of "who" you are now? How have you changed?
- Have you been able to forgive? Be specific.
- Do you feel a sense of heightened compassion?

125

What ingredients/tools seem to work best for you? Explain why.

What do you understand to have been some of your personal blocks? What is going on with them now?

What is it about this process of connection that gives you the most joy?

What have you learned about your relationships with the living and the DPs?

How do you plan to move forward?

As you arrive at this place in your practice of connecting, you have in all probability come to have a better understanding of what you have brought to your "table." You now have a clearer picture of what is in your "pantry," and what does and does not mix. I hope that you have been able to distance yourself from those things

Embrace the courage you have exhibited in coming this far.

that tend to get in your way. Now there is not only an explorer in you, but you have become an adventurer as well; you have begun to create your own banquet. Embrace the courage you have exhibited in coming this far. Celebrate your commitment to your intention to do what you wanted, and that you followed through to the best of your ability. I am proud of you!

It is important from time to time to take stock of where you are and to give yourself time to incorporate into your daily life the innovative tools you have discovered that support your sense of well-being. I encourage you to take the time to live with these new tools. Let them permeate your life so that you can see what works best for you. This is the only way you can consciously come to know if what is happening to you is what you want. Take what works and discard the rest—whether it comes from this book or some other source of support. Yet, be cautious about discarding any "tool" just because it seems a bit challenging to embrace; it might be cloaked in resistance. Take your time!

This is not a race to a finish line—it is a journey.

Having the free will to choose

If, of our own free will, we make a choice, it will have specific consequences for us. Continuing to make the same choices, and having the same consequences is called staying on the *wheel of karma*. The wheel goes around and around, and if we stay on it, we will just keep going in circles. If we

Take the risk of change.

keep repeating the same choice that keeps us angry, in denial, or resistant, then each time we will get the same unhappy result—unhappy, but not uncomfortable, since we can predict the outcome. But, we *can* choose to get off the wheel by making a different choice. Be open and willing to make another choice if an earlier one was not effective. No one is punishing you by preventing a contact; you are punishing yourself by remaining in the old mindset. As I see it, the reason for that is you are not yet ready to make contact.

So, in your desire to connect, stay open and continue to push past the urge to shutdown and declare that something is not working. The DPs bring their messages. But most often

people hear only what they want to hear. If you remain closed up or afraid, it can have a major effect on your ability to receive information that could help you to heal and move on.

You have arrived here to make contact with your loved ones *and* with yourself. Take advantage of what you have been given here, and watch yourself heal and make changes that will benefit your relation to all aspects of your life. Learn to set your own table, and present a banquet for healing. Take the risk of change. For many who have learned to listen to themselves, the rewards range from peace of mind to life-affirming joy. We all *do* have the opportunity to make contact with those who have passed over. It is our choice to take it or not. So this is a time to celebrate and acknowledge what you have accomplished, and to begin, I ask you now to revisit the letters you wrote in the beginning.

> *In the world of today, the great mystery is definitely more confrontive and in our face.*

In Chapter Two you wrote a paragraph or two to yourself in the form of a letter about what inspired you to take this path to connect. Retrieve that letter and reread what you wrote. As you read, take the time to acknowledge what you have accomplished, and journal about it.

In Chapter Three, you wrote a page to the person you wanted to contact, and about the emotions that were motivating you to do it. What has been the evolution of those initial emotions? What has developed for you in regard to making that connection? Where do you stand in your relationship with that person now? Journal this also.

Once you have allowed yourself to spend some time acknowledging what your experience has been and what you have received, give yourself permission to feel good and *celebrate* all you have done.

Since death has been the greatest mystery of all, I do believe that we are now in a period of time in terms of consciousness, tied in with technology and the world, which offers the vastness of that mystery to become smaller. In the world of today, the great mystery is definitely more confrontative and *in our face*. Practicing the tools found in this book can open the door to your own mystery.

RECIPE CARD:

 Plan a special outing to honor your progress.

 Give thanks to those loved ones who have passed over and your Higher Source for the opportunity to have had this experience.

 Journal about your transformation, specifically acknowledging your growth.

CHAPTER TEN:
Sharing Your Inner Cook with Others: Creating Support

Sharing and connecting

If you feel you are alone in this process, please know that there are a lot of you out there! One of the fruits of my labor is connecting with people from my Website, seminars, workshops, séances, one-on-one sessions, and radio shows. There is something about this sharing that creates very strong bonds. Sometimes there are no words to describe the gifts and insights found in moments of sharing—as in those "you had to have been there" situations. The sharing allows contact with the *messages* to flourish because it happens in a place of safety and understanding.

The information from connections that are sometimes realized in such intimate settings produces healing like no other—especially when the passing of a child is involved. Most of us like being with people who understand and identify with us, which is why so many of us are in book clubs, journaling, and support groups of all kinds. Sharing with those who have had similar experiences can provoke profound occurrences. The rapport and response is so valuable, often it deeply touches my heart.

I am fortunate to have just such a group on my "team" that I work with every day. A sharing group or friend is the one of the best aids to anyone's growth and healing. What you will be sharing in your practice is a very private and personal matter, as is our relationship with God, or whatever we call our Higher Source, a delicate matter to share in many cases. If you find such support, hooray for you!

My Website is a library of open sharing and information: a place for asking questions, finding and responding to books, and to many personal experiences. I invite you to visit the Message Board chat rooms on my Website at *www. suzanenorthrop.com*.

Here is an opportunity to connect with others that is definitely non-threatening as you take the step to share for the first time.

It is important that you feel protected and secure in the group or individual with whom you choose to share. Sharing in a safe environment can produce amazing insights, the most beneficial of which is finding out that *you are not alone.* It is important to build a network of "like-minded believers" when you are ready to begin to share your experiences and reveal your questions about going forward. I encourage you to be selective in your choosing. You will know when it is "right"; a special energy seems to envelope people who are gathered together for the same purpose. Remember, you have been expanding your intuitive self through your practice, so trust that inner voice.

> *It is important that you feel protected and secure in the group or individual with whom you choose to share.*

There is a host of information you can garner when you unite with others to give and receive support. Usually, when you enter a supportive atmosphere, there will be a huge leap in your progress. It also helps deepen the acceptance and understanding of what you are receiving from your contacts and messages. The reassurance that something is happening and that you are on the "right track" will be so encouraging. Solid support also gives you that boost when you find yourself frustrated and blocked because those supporting you have experienced much the same feelings of discouragement. A place of support is somewhere you can go when things don't seem to be making sense—a place where your doubts and frustrations will be validated. This in itself is profoundly healing.

Another advantage to building a support network is that whatever your feelings are at a particular moment, you get to continue the practice of acting as a "medium," to continue what you have been doing throughout this process, and learning to allow the DPs to make contact with you and through you. It also gives you the opportunity to share the tools you use to practice connecting, and to gather some new ones for yourself.

When you are with a small group that resonates with what you are doing, you also have an opportunity to practice together different ways of connecting. You can find a myriad of ideas to enhance your practice. Quite often people have discovered new approaches to take in attempting to make contact. A supportive situation provides the occasion to be free of fear about uncovering new avenues of possibilities for connecting that might not have occurred to you.

Some of the tools you can practice and observe in a group like this are how others meditate, *ask* to receive a contact, as well as other means of preparation. This can only serve to expand what you have that is working now. Of course, you also get to share what you are doing which

> **When interacting with a support group, you must keep in mind that there is no competition in this work.**

can give you a strong dose of validation. In addition, you have an opportunity to take turns "making contact" with the DPs to see what or who might come through. When you are with the group, you can practice writing down what you are receiving, and then share it for validating feedback among the group.

Another tool you can practice with a group is holding an object belonging to a member or a member's loved one, and observing what you receive. If you try this, your job is confined strictly to telling only what you are receiving. Do not analyze; just relate whatever feels significant. This can be a lot of fun and helpful to your own practice, as well. Groups can be a positive support as long as they hold to the commitment not to tell members what they *should* do. When interacting with a support group, you must keep in mind that there is no competition in this work. Its major concern must be to create a safe place where inhibitions and negative emotions can be put aside to let whatever one "gets" come through. It helps to remember that what you are doing is a privilege.

> ## No one is ever going to have all the answers.

Make no mistake. You will get information in some way.

Books also can be enormously helpful in expanding your interests and providing support. Go to a library, a bookstore, or any center of enlightenment, and see what you might be drawn to on the shelves under the categories of death, grieving, recovery, life-after-death, and the "other side." You may find that certain writings draw you in immediately, and then again, there will be others with which you do not connect at all. If you continue your search, eventually you will come upon the words and the information that seem to be written just for you. You will recognize it when it happens because it is exhilarating. Exploring such writings will help you grow. One thing to remember: each writer is speaking from his or her own experience; so, if some aspects of what is being said do not resonate with you, don't throw out the whole work. If you do, you just might miss that one "pearl" that will spur you on. No one is ever going to have all the answers.

Another avenue you might start with, if you can afford it, is to attend a lecture or seminar. In my travels, I find that they go on in most cities. There are, of course, the ones I do; you can find my up-to-date schedule in the *Calendar* section of my Website. If you are in or near New York State, The Omega Institute in Rhinebeck, NY is a great place to check out. Also, there are learning centers in most cities that offer an array of workshops and seminars on a combination of subjects that might be of interest to you as you move onward in your quest for further awareness and healing. There are also spiritual churches, centers, and philosophic groups found in most cities, even the smallest, that are open to exploring life-after-death.

A number of organizations may offer grief support in your area. Those who typically offer this resource include:

- Religious settings — churches, synagogues, mosques
- Pastoral counseling centers
- Your spiritual community—metaphysical groups that use outside facilities
- Mental health or social service agencies
- Many after-care services
- Hospices
- YMCA or similar organizations
- 12-Step support/discussion groups

In some cases, you may want to start your healing with an official support group. The following is a short list of support groups that may be available for you either in your local community or online. If you have suffered a loss, I encourage you to try to locate a support group in your area. Many are specifically about loss and can be a helpful part of the bereavement process. Comfort can be found in congregating with other bereaved families and individuals who are facing the same issues. You will find that in many cases such connections can bring friendships and life-long bonds. I have been told countless times that because of difficulties in processing the loss within their families, outside groups have offered support in a totally different way. If you don't see a support group listed for your state or local area, try starting your search with one of the national listings who's Website may be helpful.

The following are some grief-related organizations:

American Foundation for Suicide Prevention
120 Wall Street, 22nd Floor
New York, NY 10005
Phone: (212) 363-3500
Toll Free: (888) 333-AFSP
Fax: (212) 363-6237
E-Mail: inquiry@afsp.org
Website: www.afsp.org

The American Foundation for Suicide Prevention is dedicated to advancing knowledge about suicide and the ability to prevent it.

The Compassionate Friends

PO Box 3696
Oak Brook, IL 60522-3696
Phone: (630) 990-0010
Toll Free: (877) 969-0010
Website: www.compassionatefriends.org

The Compassionate Friends is a national non-profit, self-help organization that offers friendship and understanding to bereaved parents, grandparents, and siblings.

Dougy Center for Grieving Children

PO Box 86552
Portland, OR 97286
Phone: (503) 775-5683
Fax: (503) 777-3097
Website: www.dougy. org

Through their National Center for Grieving Children and Families, the Dougy Center provides support and training locally, nationally, and internationally to individuals and organizations seeking to assist grieving children and teens.

Society of Military Widows

5535 Hempstead Way
Springfield, VA 22151
Phone: (703) 750-1342
Fax: (703) 354-4380
E-Mail: naus@ix.netcom.com
Website: www.militarywidows.org

The Society of Military Widows is a nationwide organization whose purpose is to assist widows of members in all branches of uniformed services of the United States.

TAPS (Tragedy Assistance Program for Survivors), Inc.
2001 S Street, NW, Suite 300
Washington, DC 20009
Phone: (800) 959-TAPS
Fax: (202) 638-5312
Website: www.taps.org

TAPS is a national, non-profit organization serving the families and friends of those who have died while serving in the Armed Forces. Services include a military survivor peer support network, grief counseling referrals, caseworker assistance, and crisis information.

Association for Death Education and Counseling (ADEC)
342 North Main Street
West Hartford, CT 06117-2507
Phone: (860) 586-7503
Fax: (860) 586-7550
E-Mail: info@adec.org
Website: www.adec.org

ADEC is a professional organization dedicated to promoting excellence in death education, bereavement counseling, and the care of the dying.

www.Griefwatch.com

www.grieftnet.org

www.caregivers.com
A care giver virtual support group.

SHARE Organization (National)

Website: www.nationalshareoffice.com
*Services provided by SHARE are available free of charge to
bereaved parents as well as to their family and friends. It is
a tax-deductible, non-profit group. Services include support
groups and bi-monthly newsletters. Its Website has listings and
links for local SHARE groups in your area.*

MISS Foundation

Website: www.misschildren.org
*A non-profit 501(c)3 international organization providing
immediate and ongoing support to grieving families. It
helps them to empower themselves by proactive community
involvement and volunteerism, and reducing infant and toddler
death through research and education.*

UNITE

Website: www.unite.freeservers.com
*A non-profit organization in Philadelphia that provides grief
support services to families suffering from miscarriage, stillborn,
ectopic and neonatal losses.*

**The anxiety of losing a loved one
has been rooted in our fear
of death.**

Here are some online support groups:

Grief & Healing Discussion Page
Website: www.webhealing.com/cgi-bin/main.pl
An interactive Website with chat rooms for grief discussions and helpful resources.

Sidelines National Support Network
Website: www.sidelines.org/
A network of support groups around the U.S. for women with complicated and high-risk pregnancies.

The Compassionate Friends Parent Chat

Website: www.compassionatefriends.org

Chat Rooms: www.compassionatefriends.org/Chat/chat_entrances.shtml

A network of chat rooms specifically for bereaved parents, siblings and family members. A schedule of chat times can be found on the main web site.

... the true riches in life lie within.

www.suzanenorthrop.com

A message board of chat rooms concerned with loved ones who have passed over and about making contact. I have spoken about my Website earlier in the beginning of the chapter. Please visit us.

As a final note, I want to encourage you to continue to search for the ways you can begin to build support—whether it is turning to a trusted friend, family member, or group. If none of

those seem to work in the beginning, then seek a professional to help you to validate what you are feeling, seeking, and receiving as you do this work. You have an opportunity now to concretize what you have been learning by bringing it into the "open." It is strictly up to you to decide when the time is right—and when the setting is safe.

The anxiety of losing a loved one has been rooted in our fear of death. We have been raised in a culture that fears death, hides it from us, giving us the strong and recurrent sense of things not working out as we planned. Most of our anger and pain come from an underlying knowledge that we have no control over this. It is also true, however, that death and the feeling of hopelessness can be a motivation for searching out a new way of thinking, particularly about life-after-death. Our grief can propel us into learning to live an insightful, compassionate life—a life that is more in touch with our soul's journey and its healing.

To begin this journey, we each had to start from a place of hopelessness, frustration, grief, and a feeling of not being able to come to grips with our losses. You have taken a step toward healing more than just your loss. Honor yourself for that.

I would like to close this chapter with the following message found in Jeffrey Moses' *Oneness*:

> *Life is structured so that the finest, most meaningful aspects are often hidden from outer exposure. The sweetness of an orange is hidden within a bitter skin. The seed of a tree, from which life will spring, is protected within a hard shell. And a [person] may walk the earth, not knowing that a vast depository*

of riches lies hidden deep within the ground beneath [their] feet.

From earliest childhood our senses respond to outward sensations. Without guidance and understanding, we could spend a lifetime appreciating the world only in an outward direction. But the true riches in life lie within.

You have chosen to explore the riches within, and now, with an expanded sense of self, you can step out, voice your truth, and claim your healing. *Namasté* —the light in me welcomes the light in you.

RECIPE CARD:

 How do you feel about sharing your experiences? What would you like to share?

 Where might you begin to find support?

 What "riches" have you discovered in yourself?

CHAPTER ELEVEN

Enjoying the Dessert:
Having an Attitude of Gratitude

G ratitude, one of the greatest attributes one can possess By now you have come to understand a lot more about connecting with those loved ones who have passed over. With your consistent practice, and the broadening of your support base, there ought to be a *new sense of self* permeating your life. Also, it is probably noticeable to your friends and family. Now that is something to be grateful for!

When you began to open up and share your experiences with others, it is most likely that you also began to build an extended family of relationships that work for you. It is highly probable that as a result of practicing your tools, you have seen some amazing resolutions occur in your present relationships—not to mention those with the loved one who has passed over. I imagine that, as you continue to use your tools for connection, your practice, because you know it supports your well-being and self-awareness, is by now a daily ritual you have come to cherish.

Sometimes in the process of attaining a new sense of self and family, we don't necessarily care what other people think. We have a certain confidence continuously building inside. It still doesn't mean, however, that we cannot be hurt by our families' and friends' comments, which is why our new "family" is so important to us at times. Within their midst we can find the encouragement we need to keep going and to be validated for what we are doing. In such an atmosphere, we can continue to grow and enrich our lives and our connections.

This is the time to enjoy the "dessert." As you go along with your practice and new support, there will be an accumulation of many fond memories, as well as ties to old

ones. Since we are talking about desserts, I have a wonderful memory—connection—to my Grandmother every time I eat or even think of lemon meringue pie. I remember how delicious a treat it was and how loving my Grandmother was. That memory showers me with a warm feeling all over and I know I have just had a connection with her. I trust that you have also come to realize how many different ways there are to connect with those loved ones who have passed over. Exciting, isn't it? As long as you stay open, you have the opportunity to receive messages in any moment. This is one of the greatest gifts of continuing your practice. In this context, you can have all the calories your life can handle without gaining weight!

> **As long as you stay open, you have the opportunity to receive messages in any moment.**

Following the path of expansion that we are engaged in gives you an opportunity to turn destructive patterns that have been operating in your life into constructive springboards for creating the life you desire—one that is not ruled by blame, anger, or shame. You will learn to live fully in a Universe that supports you as never before. You will find that the energy that comes from the inner peace and quiet that you have gained will ripple through all that you do. Don't get me wrong, I am not saying that everything is going to be rosy. What I am saying is that your approach to people and situations that were agitating for you before, you will meet now with a different understanding and energy. You will move from a conditioned reaction to an action that comes from not having to do battle or prove anything. You will no longer have to explain yourself to be validated.

Another gift I hope you have learned to be grateful for is the time you have set aside to be alone. It is one of the most precious of gifts I have ever given myself. I know that each of us has heard the "call" to come to silence especially in times of loss. We can learn so much by taking time to be with ourselves. For those who are not used to doing this, I know it can be uncomfortable at first. Yet, if you have persevered, I am sure that you have come to see it as a necessity for your well-being and self-discovery. I hope, too, by spending more time with yourself that you have been inspired to create more solitude in your life and to value it highly. I expect that you have also discovered that creating solitude for yourself does not also mean that people will be absent in your life; on the

"What a lovely surprise to finally discover how un-lonely being alone can be." –Ellen Burstyn, Broadway and film actress

contrary, you will start enjoying people more. When we give ourselves permission to "be still" inside long enough, we can finally begin to feel fully what our emotions are and to be aware of what we really know. Our doubts, fears, labels and automatic responses—those negative voices—will eventually ebb away. We can then become the one who experiences and not the one to whom experiences are given.

In taking time to practice the ingredients offered you in this book, you cannot help but come to know yourself better. You will have a greater understanding of your relationships with people and things. You also will learn that most of the doubts people have about what you are trying to do are theirs, not yours. You will be reaching toward forgiving yourself as well as others, and I cannot reiterate too often, *forgiveness is the greatest healer of all.*

Silence coupled with meditation is one of the most spiritual of disciplines, and I can promise you, the rewards are like the most delicious dessert we can imagine.

If you took time to carefully look into the ingredients or tools you are drawn to, I am sure you have opened the doors to making connections—to yourself and your loved ones. When you open yourself to new ways of connecting, you receive the gift of returning to the love that has always been there, and the chance to realize that life—and your soul—is in an endless cycle of change. I hope you have begun to understand that you have not been separated from the one who has passed over, but that your relation to him or her has changed. Pay attention to those ingredients that work best for you, and remember to stay open to messages coming from anywhere and anything. Be grateful for your awareness and be steadfast in it and you will not be disappointed. As long as you remain in a receptive mode, your new awareness will "signal" a contact. You are taking a great leap inward *and* beyond.

Trust, as we have said, is a big component in making contact with those who have passed over. Trusting the information you receive allows more of it to be revealed. If you have set yourself up for success, you will have it. Learning to trust in what you are doing and what you are receiving is paramount to widening your realm of connections. You are now operating at an amplified level of communication. Be grateful for that. You are developing a sixth sense, giving you a greater depth and breadth of communication. As you continue to practice, thinking narrowly

> *. . . forgiveness is the greatest healer of all.*

will become less attractive to you. The transition into a higher state of consciousness will take on a new meaning and give you new energy and you will come to a new appreciation of yourself. This is the way of the Master Chef.

As you proceed, I hope that your impression of death as *the end* has begun to transform, and that you are beginning to realize that it is not an end at all. The loss is hard, but by believing that those loved ones who pass over are not gone, we can continue to have a beautiful relationship with them. I am always amazed at how some children look at death. I remember one eleven-year-old boy, who, when asked if he knew where his grandmother had gone, gave this reply. "Oh yes, she is out there. She has just taken her space suit off." Surely he sensed she was still around, just not in the same costume.

If you plan to share your newfound "recipes for connection" with your family, just be aware that when you impart information that you receive, there might be something that comes through that does not make sense to you. It may very well occur because you are not aware of some family secrets or skeletons. These may have the potential to create conflicts, so do not judge or analyze the information. Furthermore, do not question what you receive because those questions eventually will become doubts. Just be grateful for what you

> *It isn't always easy bringing clarity to a situation or relationship . . .*

receive and pass it on. You will probably come to understand it later as a result, perhaps, of a confidential moment with a family member. It isn't always easy bringing clarity to a situation or relationship, especially if there are unresolved issues remaining.

You have learned, also, that journaling is not only a great companion, but one that also provides insight. By staying with the writing as you go on so much can be revealed and discovered. I hope that after journaling for a while, the editing ego has begun to take a backseat and the information that is meant just for you is coming to the front. Those innermost thoughts and messages will become evident to you as you read and reread your journals. How transforming this exercise can be! So, keep on journaling and continue keeping your journals in a safe place.

If you have been journaling your dreams, you probably realize by now that they are among the safest ways the DPs have of connecting with us. Unfortunately we have been taught to disregard our dreams as fantasy, merely the work of the imagination, and just so much hogwash. Yet, dreaming and dreams are sure avenues of connections with our loved ones. Stay with them, and even consider participating in some dream workshops. Dreams are loaded with symbolism, and the messages received through them can be quite profound. Daydreaming can also produce a connection to messages being sent. Don't be afraid of your dreams—day or night.

... dreaming and dreams are sure avenues of connections with our loved ones.

There are several other ingredients I hope you have been incorporating into your practice. Music should bring strong associations that will produce connections. Allow this type of practice to continue taking you to expanded territories of receiving. It can trigger contacts that can send you straight to the heart of your innermost self. Music, after all, is the universal language. Also, going out and surrounding yourself with nature should be a mandatory activity by now; if you have made it one, it can be a blessing. Enjoying what nature offers us enables us to connect to our souls—and there are few activities that can do this for us. What a wonderful way to connect to the abundance of the Universe. If you have doubts about this, start counting the leaves on a tree or bush, the blades of grass, or the grains of sand on a beach. How could you not see that we have a wildly abundant existence?

Seek out art and enjoy it. Art can speak to us in so many different ways, and carries with it so many different embedded messages. You may never know who might be "speaking" to you through a piece of art, whether it is your own or done by someone else. Learn to look at art with an open heart. By now you have learned that movement gets you up and out of your sedentary rut. Once you begin to move the body, in any way at all, the rest of you also comes alive. So, I encourage you to continue to get up and out more because movement activates not just the body, but also the spirit. When you are animated you are in contact with the soul; the soul, in turn, becomes connected to all there is to embrace in your existence. You know by now that it so important to regularly incorporate celebration into your life. Creating ceremony around your achievements helps you to hold on fast to their sacredness. You know that there are special

> *Art can speak to us in so many different ways, and carries with it so many different embedded messages.*

times, meals, and occasions that spark memories—ones that sometimes fill you with anxiety. Now is the time you need to

create new celebrations and rituals that will bring a host of good memories for you. When gratitude comes to my mind, I can't help but think of the incredible life I have supporting people in so many ways: in healing, in returning to love, and, of course, in connecting with loved ones. I feel certain that if you embrace the ingredients I have offered in this book, you, too, will enjoy the adventure of "cooking up" your connections.

I would like to believe that you have come to a greater understanding of *who* you are and what you need to support your Soul Program. I would like to believe also that you have begun to tap into the power of the explorer in yourself. Life is an adventure, and we have been given a fabulous "kitchen" in the Universe for the evolution of our souls. The soul's essence exists everywhere and is present without limit. You just have to open up to the possibility of it. Once you realize that we are in constant and never-ending evolution, then you will know that nothing ceases to exist. I am grateful that you have come to these pages, and that you have taken the risk to explore. If you have put your heart into this effort, I am sure you have not been disappointed. Congratulations!

The soul's essence exists everywhere and is present without limit.

I would like you to take some time to acknowledge in your journal what has happened and what you plan to do as you go forward.

What positive action have you taken to change during this process and what results have you noticed?

What has given you the most pleasure? What has been the most challenging?

What changes have you been able to make to shift your way of thinking? Try to be specific. Are there issues you have resolved with a loved one in a current relationship or with one who has passed over?

Our approach to life and death determines the way we experience those states. The decisions we make, not merely the conditions of our lives, gives us our destiny. If we decide we are going to be loving, forgiving, and grateful, we *will* be. If we continue to believe that we can make contact, we will. What it takes is belief and commitment. Intention sets the direction we want our lives to take and what we desire for ourselves. If that intention is not clear, we will find it is easier to fall into unwanted patterns of behavior

> *The decisions we make, not merely the conditions of our lives, gives us our destiny.*

and to have a quality of life that is much less than we deserve— that is to say, we will be led aimlessly by the beliefs and doubts of others. As we have learned, when we act differently we get different results.

Above all, be grateful—grateful for *all* the relationships in your life. They are opportunities for growth and healing that ultimately return us to the path of love. With what you have experienced here, I hope you have shifted some of the patterns of doubt, pain, and discontent that have kept you in a sense of despair. In doing that I trust that you have come to understand that the words we use to describe situations, others, and ourselves shape our beliefs. So, speak to others the way you want to be

Never underestimate the power of gratitude . . .

spoken to, say what you mean, and speak of what you believe can happen. The beliefs you consistently hold will create your future. When we embrace the energy of change, we can transform every area of our lives from our sense of self-worth to the way we deal with the world at large—and even the world beyond. Never underestimate the power of gratitude: be grateful for what you have been able to do, and be excited about what is ahead. And remember, nothing is impossible, the impossible just takes a little longer.

RECIPE CARD:

 What are you most grateful for today?

 Have you been able to reach out in forgiveness? To whom and about what?

 For the next week, write down three things you are grateful for each morning before you start the day.

CHAPTER TWELVE:
From Cook to Chef: Where to Go Next

Checking in before stepping out

As we come to this last chapter and you consider what to do and where to go next, I ask you to keep in mind that the journey has just begun. The path of conscious expansion you are on now is a perpetual one once you start. Some days you will wish that you could go back to being *unaware*, but once you have opened that door to *connecting* there is no closing it—and, that is a blessing. To live an unconscious existence only keeps us in denial and in a self-imposed state of naiveté, the consequences of which we have all seen in this world today. It does not serve our higher good and our growth to pretend we do not know what we need to do for our soul's program, and for our relationships—past and present. We have known all along, we have just kept it at bay by refusing to address what pains us. You are now on a path to enlightenment—a path of love in the highest regard. Continuing to search for people, places, associations, elements, and situations that can support your growth is critical to building bridges of love, compassion, and forgiveness. And it is marvelous that your feeling of self-worth benefits also. You will find as you go along that souls with like energy do find one another, whether on this plane, the next one, or between the two. Our souls always know where they need to be because, as science has now taught us, energy exists at all points simultaneously in the space-time continuum.

One can never know where a message from a loved one might appear. While the vibrating pull of those suffering similar losses may be the strongest kind of bonding glue, the fact is that anyone who has suffered a loss and is trying to communicate with a loved one in spirit will be, to some degree, drawn to others who are doing the same. When I do retreats, seminars, or cruises during which people are of necessity together for an extended period of time, I find that there are always bonding experiences. It can also be healing simply because the people there are "in the same kitchen," either literally or figuratively, and they can provide solace and comfort for one another. Sometimes, I feel sure the DPs have arranged it that way.

We are always drawn to one another because one of us has something to teach the other, we both have something to learn, or because the situation created by our meeting will help the soul to grow and move on to the next level of its development. So, I encourage you to continue to seek out those who may become a support. Each soul has its *earthly* lessons to learn. Although these lessons may be as various as our Soul Programs are, you can be sure there is always a reason for them. Situations do occur in which we have been trying to resolve issues or learn a lesson from another soul and have not been able to get it right despite long and hard efforts. If that is the case, and if continuing to do the same thing over and over seems to be getting you nowhere, by the "gift of grace," you will learn what you need to know in some other way. To learn about love is one of the basic reasons we are here, and when we are asked to learn that lesson through loss, it can be most challenging.

The DPs want those they have left behind to make the choices that will help them move on in their soul's program, and the *Power* in charge of the "team upstairs" wants those in spirit to do

> **Each soul has its earthly lessons to learn.**

the same. That is why whatever unfinished aspect any one soul needs to complete in its program will get done—one way or the other. The basic lessons for all of us to learn are the giving and receiving of love; being able to do that is essential to everyone's life. I believe that reading this book and moving through the process have brought many of you to a time of decision. Will you remain satisfied living from now on in a space of denial, ignorance, and unresolved issues? I trust you will say, "No." This is a time that is calling each and every one of you to live with a deep dedication to your loved ones, relationships, your life, and yourselves. You are excitingly on the threshold from the old to the new, from dark to light, from illusion to truth, and from complacency to adventure. No doubt there is a reason for having found yourself where you are at this moment in time—you have brought yourself to it.

You have been given a way, in these pages, to make some changes in your life and how you live it. It is quite possible that the pain of a loss is what brought you here. When we are in such acute pain, we most often breakdown, but within that breakdown is a gift. Once we breakdown, we are most likely to breakup, and from a breakup, we are in position for a breakthrough. This is shorthand for the following scenario: you *break down* into the pain of loss, then you *break apart* in that space, and the next thing—if you become aware—is

To learn about love is one of the basic reasons we are here . . .

that you have a choice to *break through* to a new understanding and conscious awareness, leaving the "old self and old thinking" behind. These are the moments that change lives. And, the good news is that you have been doing your work to become more consciously aware and the "dessert" is there for you to experience. This is when you come to the joy of the banquet table. We are in this life for a purpose—whether we are aware of it or not. We are here to accomplish what each soul has chosen as its program—whatever our souls need to learn. It might be patience or self-reliance or dealing with loss or compassion. Each soul has a different program, and there lies the reason never to compare your progress with anyone else's. The soul's path is to grow, but how each path grows is unique to each soul.

As you bravely continue in your kitchen to explore the recipes that serve you well, I believe you will come to realize that you actually live a dual existence. There are two selves at play here. There is the self of the personality and all its earthly expressions and the higher, endless, invisible, immeasurable self—your *Soul Self*. The Earth's program is difficult. That is why we learn so much. Sometimes the learning comes from experiences created by the personality, and not the person. When we are born, the personality is born also, for that particular lifetime; since we will have free will as well as personality, the soul's choices have been set by the soul's program for that lifetime. The Soul Self, or individual soul, is like a planet in the total *Universe of Cosmic Life* that we call the "Soul of God" or the "Oversoul." Working on the Soul Program, we have the prospect of growing and expanding our energy and consciousness to become more and more like the Oversoul or God Consciousness. This is the evolution of the Soul. It does not

> **Sometimes the learning comes from experiences created by the personality, and not the person.**

matter if you were skeptical in regard to what you were about to approach in these pages. Being a healthy skeptic is a good thing. Yet, I know that if you surrender to examining the things that happen in your life and why they might happen, you will begin to see, hear, touch, and

> ***You have been doing your work, so trust your intuition.***

experience life from a different perspective. Besides making the contacts that you wish to make, you might just come to know yourself as you really are.

As you go forward, I support you in seeking out those who will help you stay on course. If you decide to look to a professional, here are a few things to keep in mind. One of the best ways to start is to find a person in your support group who might recommend someone to you. It helps to eliminate that "stab in the dark" approach. He or she can also give you some insight into how the professional works. If it is a one-on-one situation, see if you can have a chat with the professional before you sign up so that you can "feel" if his or her energy is right for you. You have been doing your work, so trust your intuition. Don't compare one professional to another if possible, we all have our different personalities and do our work in various ways. In the beginning, it is probably safer to go to a seminar to observe how the individual delivers information and interacts with contacts—the DPs. Then, if you connect with this professional and if he or she offers a retreat or workshop, sign up and give it a try. Whatever else does or does not happen, you might, at the least, meet some new people to bond with or obtain information about where to investigate next.

There are a large variety of good practitioners to choose from these days, however, as happens in any profession, a few bad apples may turn up. That is why seminars may be a good place to find out if the medium "rings a bell" with you before taking the next step. If someone recommends a medium, it is important you not only trust the person who is giving the recommendation, but helpful if you share similar values. I think that recommendations are an excellent means of exploring a profession, nonetheless, in keeping with my own professional philosophy, I will not recommend someone I have not worked with or know their work personally. I would suggest that you wait for the professional who is *right* for you rather than rushing into a disappointing experience that may leave a very bad taste of "medium" in your mouth. After all, you are in a vulnerable state, fragile, and most likely in the early stage of your loss and striking out on your own. You want this experience to be a loving one and as uplifting as possible—the very reason that some mediums require waiting for a time after a death before giving a session. The first stages of a grieving state, I strongly believe, may not be the best time for you to pursue this avenue of connection. That is why the suggestion to attend seminars and lectures to begin with is warranted. Of course, most of us want private sessions, so here is what to expect: many well-known mediums may be expensive, expect it. Many do not do private sessions at all, only seminars, groups, or workshops. What they charge is based, as a rule, on the type of session and how much in demand they are. Once more you will want to trust your intuition.

Stay with what works

Now you have some tips on how to continue to search for and build support outside your immediate experiences. To add a final note on this, I want to strongly encourage you to keep connected to what *has* been working for you. Stay with your practice, and share with those who you have found to be sensitive to what you are doing. Let this arena be the one where you explore new tools, and experiences. If you have entered a small group and it is giving you a great deal of

> *... keep connected to what has been working for you.*

assistance, continue with it. If you have already connected with a professional on a one-on-one basis, and had a great session—got a connection—wonderful. But, as you continue doing this on your own, when something is working well for you, just keep on developing that situation or tool to see where it takes you. As I have said before, you will know when something is "right" for you. The newly anchored spiritual explorer in you is your friend, your ally. Trust in that connection and go forward. My wish for you is that you continue to have wonderful and safe experiences of connecting.

RECIPE CARD:

 Make a list of new possibilities to explore.

 Find a seminar or workshop to attend.

 Review your *Commitment Contract* and set a new commitment for yourself and your practice.

Epilogue

It is my hope that after reading this book you will have much more than just a glimmer of how to make your own connections, and that you have gathered together some tools to help you open those doors. From my beginning as a working professional medium, the element of my practice that has been the most meaningful, besides the messages, is helping others open up and explore their own connections. Once someone knows that contacts happen, and discovers how they happen, understanding begins to reveal itself about his or her own Soul Journey, and that everything does happen for a reason.

Every time I have looked into a mother, father, sister, brother, or friend's face and heard some of them say they have not received any contact from their loved one, I have gently said, "I am sure you have, but you just haven't been able to recognize or know the way or ways contact may have happened." So, it is from the look of loss in every one of those faces that I have drawn my inspiration to write "A Medium's Cookbook: recipes for the soul," a book of recipes showing how to explore the journey of opening your heart and soul to a banquet of ways to connect to your loved one. I speak to you personally from my own heart and grief. I understand what it is like to feel that "hole" in your heart and to want it filled. It has been comforting for me to know without question that someone who has passed over is safe, loved, and near to our hearts. That is why writing my last book *Everything Happens for a Reason* was so profound and significant an experience. But, I could not know the impact the words of my title would have and how true they would "ring" for me in my own experience. I, like so many of you, have been challenged throughout my life by these words—this phrase—having had many personal losses, tests, and painfully eye-opening experiences. A loss I was yet to go through would put me to the test once more.

On January 26, 2004, my beloved nephew, Aaron, passed over. He passed one month before his twenty-fourth birthday on a very cold winter's day. It remains a shock still. Although unable, even after some time had gone by, to believe this, I know unquestioningly that he is as free as a butterfly. Grieving, I saw in my mind's eye the face of every parent and of others I have seen over the years who have gone through such a loss—all of us wanting a second chance to connect or to know that our loved ones are well, out of pain, and that the love continues. Children have always held a very special place for me in my work. A few months before Aaron's passing, I had an almost obsessive urge to connect with children, and I was sought out to lecture in organizations whose work was concerned with children's deaths. At one of these events, months after Aaron's passing, I heard a woman say in an odd tone to another woman I knew had also lost her son, "Now Suzane knows how we feel." I knew in my heart that what she was saying was not meant to be malicious; it was another's pain shouting out over her own devastating loss.

What I clung to during the months after Aaron's death, even in my grief and the feeling that my insides had been ripped out, was the certainty that he would contact me. And, I almost knew how it would happen. To my delight, I have had so many contacts with him and so have many other friends and family members as well. I have been blessed by this connection and its continuation since his death. This does not end my missing him, or the loss of not being able to hold him, or not being able to see what his life journey on this "earth place" would have been. These are normal and natural desires for us because we live in the physical world. But what I do know is that we are so much more than our bodies. Our essence/spirit/soul *does* live on. In saying this, I want you to understand that I do not take any of this earthly journey lightly. It is a very important and beautiful journey. For that reason, if for nothing else, I want to do all I can to help each of you open wonderful doors of connection to your loved ones, to yourself, to your own heart and soul, and to the hearts and souls of our precious DPs.

I would like you to come to know, as I do, that we are never alone in our loss, although it may seem so. If you reach out and connect, somewhere there will be an ear, an understanding heart, or support waiting and ready to reach back. Enjoy the many recipes that are waiting to happen, setting those tables, and presenting your meals. Whether it is with your DPs or the living, what awaits you is the gift of sharing your banquet of life and love.

Works Cited

Animal-Speak: The Spiritual & Magical Powers of Creatures Great & Small
Llewellyn Publishing, 1st ed edition, October 1993

Animal Wisdom by Jessica Dawn Palmer,
Thorsons Publishers, July 2001

The Artist's Way: A Spiritual Path to Higher Creativity
Tarcher; 10th annv edition, March 2002

Changing Course: Healing from Loss, Abandonment, and Fear by Claudia Black,
Hazeldon, February 2002

Heart Land by Tim Wheater,
Audio CD, October 1995

Medicine Cards: The Discovery of Power Through the Ways of Animals by Jamie Sams,
David Carson, Angela C. Werneke,
St. Martin's Press, Rev Bk & Crd edition, July 1999

Oneness: Great Principles Shared by All Religions by Jeffrey Moses,
Ballantine Books, Revised and Expanded Edition, October 2002

The Healing Energies of Music by Hal A. Lingerman,
Quest Books, 2nd edition, May 1995

The Woman's Book of Dreams: Dreaming As a Spiritual Practice by Connie Cockrell
Kaplan,
Beyond Words Publishing, May 1999

About the Author

Suzane Northrop

is recognized nationally and worldwide as a trance medium and expert in psychic phenomena. She discovered her "gift" as a young child, and for over 30 years has been using that gift to help bridge the gap between the world of the living and the spirit world. Suzane brings a unique contribution to the ever-growing body of literature by and about those who communicate with souls who have passed over to another plane. Rather than simply relating stories gleaned from her work, she has made it her mission to convey her understanding that each of us is here on earth, in this lifetime, for a reason, and that reason is to complete a particular portion of what will be a never-ending Soul Journey.

In her first and second books, *Second Chance: Healing Messages from the Afterlife*, and *Everything Happens for a Reason: Love, Free Will, and the Lessons of the Soul*, Suzane shares her journey of discovery, acceptance, and guidance through life with the Dead Peoples' Society; a term she lovingly calls DPs. Suzane has toured extensively in the United States and has lectured in Great Britain at the British Society for Psychic Research. She has helped thousands through her seminars and private séances contact loved ones who have passed over, bringing relief and clarity to what lies beyond our time here on Earth.

Suzane's amazing and accurate abilities have been showcased in numerous radio and television appearances, such as *Extra, Entertainment Tonight,* and *Access Hollywood.* Other appearances include specials on MSNBC, Fox Family Channel, and The Discovery

Channel. Suzane was also a participant in an HBO documentary, entitled *Life After Life,* in which research was conducted into the study of consciousness surviving life-after-death.

Suzane is on staff at Omega Institute, and The Crossings in Austin, Texas, and has been a guest lecturer at Scripps Integrated Medicine conferences in Hawaii.

Suzane has hosted her own radio talk show in New York, and is excited about her up and coming syndicated radio show.

You can learn more about Suzane Northrop and her upcoming events by visiting her Website at www.suzanenorthrop.com.

Other books by Suzane Northrop:

Everything Happens for a Reason: Love, Free Will, and the Lessons of the Soul

Second Chance: Healing Messages from the Afterlife

Northstar 2 Publishing
New York, New York

Notes

Notes